Inside racist Europe

by

Liz Fekete and
Frances Webber

with an introduction by
A. Sivanandan

Institute of Race Relations
2-6 Leeke Street, London WC1X 9HS

This report is based on the first eighteen months' work of the Institute of Race Relations European Race Audit. *Liz Fekete* is full-time researcher on the Audit. *Frances Webber* is a barrister and member of the Institute of Race Relations Council.

We should like to thank the Joseph Rowntree Charitable Trust and the European Commission for their support for the Audit and for this report.

We should also like to thank all those individuals who have contributed to the work of the European Race Audit, but especially Leena-Kaisa Åberg, Saba Bahar, Matthew Carr, Phil Collins, Joe Frank, Britta Grell, Stefanie Lay, Cath Mersh and Chris Woodall for their sustained work over the course of the project.

Published by the Institute of Race Relations
2-6 Leeke Street, London WC1X 9HS
© Institute of Race Relations 1994
ISBN 085001 045 4

Cover design by Mick Keates
Typeset by Nancy White
Printed by the Russell Press, Nottingham

Contents

Introduction

Racism is no longer about racial or cultural superiority. No race is held to be biologically superior to another, other cultures do not necessarily 'swamp' one's own. Racism is about prosperity, and prosperity is white, western, European. The asylum-seeker, refugee, immigrant is invariably non-white, or, if white, non-prosperous, unsettled, an itinerant from Eastern Europe. The point is to keep them out. The democratic way of doing that is to criminalise them first – through the due process of law.

The whole European programme on immigration, from the setting up of the secretive Trevi group of police chiefs and ministers of the interior to the hush-hush talks of heads of state in Schengen and Edinburgh and Dublin, has been an exercise in creating laws and regulations that would strip immigrants of all legality before they are either refused entry or deported. And if the legal argument does not work, there is always the economic: they are not coming here for asylum, but to take our jobs, our homes, our wealth.

Over and above the common European policies and programmes to criminalise the immigrant, each country also has its own traditional way of excluding immigrants either from the country or, if within the country, from that country's citizenship. Thus, Germany excludes you by simply not making you a citizen, never mind that you were born and bred there; France, by denying the automatic right to citizenship to those who formerly had it. In Italy, you could get deported if you are arrested for theft, arson or damage to property, even before standing trial, let alone being found guilty. In Switzerland, they are going to make it illegal for you to step outside your canton.

Together, these form the strands of a Euro-culture of popular racism, which stereotypes all Third World/Black immigrants as terrorists and drug-runners and all Eastern European/White immigrants as thieves and shoplifters.

This book, however, is not written from the perspective of the rise of the secret European state, unaccountable to all but its officials. Nor is it, directly, an account of the common, market racism which sets the agenda for the European Right and stokes the fires of fascism. It is, first and foremost, a stark, straightforward record of how the new Euro-racism, institutionalised in the laws of the European Union and broadcast by the popular press, maims and kills its victims, disfigures the victimiser and contorts our civilisation.

This report, which forms the annual volume of the Institute of Race Relations' ongoing European Race Audit, is the first of its kind and owes not a little to the support and good offices of the Joseph Rowntree Charitable Trust, who had the imagination to fear for the future.

A. Sivanandan
Director, Institute of Race Relations

1 Inside racist Europe

In 1991, the Institute of Race Relations warned that the structures to close Europe to immigrants and refugees were being secretly set in place by the Trevi* group of ministers and police chiefs and the inter-state treaty makers of Schengen.[1] Furthermore, it warned, the role of Schengen and Trevi, as well as of the Ad Hoc Group on Immigration, was not only to create a hard outer barrier to prevent asylum-seekers and immigrants from entering fortress Europe, but also to develop mechanisms of internal control that would effectively police those 17 million people, mostly black and Third World, settled in Europe but without citizens' rights.

The rationale for the creation of forums like Trevi was the shifting, in the post cold-war period, of Western Europe's security concerns from the external Soviet 'threat' to the 'terrorist' threat within. And, as Europe perceived itself as more vulnerable once border controls were reduced, the 'internal' threat loomed that much larger. Increasingly, the source of that internal threat, as witnessed by Trevi's preoccupations with all the 'security and policing aspects of freedom of movement', is seen as the non-citizen within Europe's borders. Hence, this audit will focus on the different ways in which this racist conflation of issues has worked itself out in practice across Europe. For, secretive though the decision-making of Trevi and the Ad Hoc Group on Immigration might be, its effects are becoming manifest across Europe in: agreements between police forces to 'cooperate' over the detention and deportation of 'undesirables'; the harmonisation of exclusion processes for asylum-seekers; and police operations to identify and deport 'illegal' workers, carried out, inevitably, in a context of saturation policing of 'immigrant' areas. All of which is underpinned by the compilation of racially

* Trevi is an acronym for terrorism, radicalism, extremism and violence. Since its forma-tion in 1976, the Trevi group has expanded its remit to embrace 'all the policing and security aspects of free movement', including immigration, visas, asylum-seekers and border controls.

classified crime statistics, which, in turn, are used to fuel media campaigns against 'immigrant crime'.

THE NON-CITIZEN AS SUSPECT

Crime, the press and the police

If the security services and police chiefs, huddled in these secretive and non-accountable forums, have helped create a whole new array of suspects, it is Europe's media, through their fixation with immigrant and refugee crime (in popular consciousness the two are often collapsed), that have given substance to the shadowy stereotypes outlined by Trevi. Furthermore, in some instances, police chiefs have legitimised media stereotypes about immigrants through the release of crime statistics that seek to prove that immigrants and asylum-seekers are disproportionately involved in crime. In **Germany**, where the federal commissioner for alien affairs has warned against the general use of the notion of 'foreign criminality', a police trade union leader, Hermann Lutz, made the amazing claim in August 1993 that asylum-seekers were responsible for 10 per cent of all crime in Germany and 33 per cent of all crime carried out by foreigners.[2]

In September 1991, in the **Netherlands**, the minister of the interior initiated a 'National Debate on Ethnic Minorities' which seems to have been interpreted by both the police and media as inaugurating a debate on immigrants and crime. The police commissioner for Amsterdam, for instance, made a series of unsubstantiated public statements accusing illegal Ghanaian workers of being responsible for crime in the city.[3]

Then, in November 1992, a much-publicised story about Turkish immigrant welfare scroungers was shown to be totally without foundation. The mayor of Rotterdam, Mr A Peper, backed by the police, had made a statement to the effect that members of the Turkish community were involved in large-scale security frauds. Rotterdam city council and the local police were later challenged to prove a claim that 110 Turks had registered for social security at one address and were collecting benefits to send back to Turkey. No proof was forthcoming, so, in order to expose this falsehood, several anti-racist organisations put an advert into the local paper condemning Mr Peper's statement and apologising to Rotterdam's Turkish community.[4]

Again, in late January 1993, the police commissioner for Amsterdam released crime statistics that purported to prove that youth from Surinam and the Dutch Antilles were heavily over-represented in street robberies. The police commissioner went on to call for the building of more police cells to deal with the crisis and the media warned of 'LA-style riots'.

The Antillean minister of justice, S Romer, visited the Netherlands for talks with her Dutch counterpart. She warned that it was dangerous to employ stereotypes, particularly at a time of growing racism. She also pointed out that, whereas there were all sorts of Dutch drug dealers in Antillean prison cells, this did not lead Antilleans to stereotype all Dutch as drug dealers.[5]

*　　*　　*

Both media and police scare-stories are used by politicians to justify projected legislative change. Denmark offers an example of the way this can build up, and also shows the links between the stigmatising of refugees as 'freeloaders' and the increase in racist attacks on them.

In **Denmark**, throughout October 1992, the press focused on the problem of petty crime, particularly shoplifting, amongst asylum-seekers, which led to shopkeepers in Gram imposing a short-lived ban on foreigners bringing bags into their shops. On 20 October, Danish TV's *45 minutes* programme visited the town of Gråsten. The programme, which was criticised for its highly negative format, showed that the recent arrival of refugees from the former Yugoslavia had resulted in bar and shop owners refusing to serve them and in local people claiming that the new arrivals would cream off social benefits and jobs. Some people interviewed also threatened demonstrations to protest against the government's asylum policies.

In this climate, Danish youth, who petrol-bombed a refugee centre in Gram in October 1992, justified their action by claiming that their attack was to punish shoplifters. Another youth, who assaulted two asylum-seekers from the former Yugoslavia, told a court in February 1993 that he was against Yugoslavs coming to Denmark and sponging off society.[6]

Negative reporting continued in 1993, with detailed press coverage of refugee criminality, usually shoplifting cases, despite the fact that there is no evidence that the level of shoplifting is higher amongst refugees than Danes. Nevertheless, the damage had been done, public opinion prejudiced. An opinion poll carried out in June 1993 found that 88 per cent of the Danish population believe that 'criminal asylum-seekers' should be immediately deported.[7]

Indeed, in June 1993, following a highly-publicised case of shoplifting by nine refugees from the former Yugoslavia in Tarm, mid-

Jutland, a Liberal MP called for the deportation of any asylum-seeker found guilty of a criminal offence. Interior minister Birte Weiss rejected the call, but did accept that the applications of asylum-seekers found guilty of a criminal offence should be dealt with with greater speed.[8] In its most recent pronouncement, the Liberal Party has called for the introduction of closed refugee camps for the internment of violent asylum-seekers.

Another clear example of the police/media/immigrant crime build-up leading to political intervention is seen in **Norway**.

In March 1993, the police in Oslo released crime statistics that sought to prove that immigrants were over-represented in crimes of violence, rape, assault and robbery. Following this, and a media focus on 'immigrant crime', prime minister Brundtland issued a seven-point programme against crime which included the proposal that there should be a stricter process of selection for asylum and more information for 'foreigners' on Norwegian laws and culture.

The proposals were made in the run-up to the September 1993 elections. Thus, 'law and order' became a hotly-debated political issue, with the debate focusing almost exclusively on immigrants and crime. The leader of the Conservative Party, Kaci Kullmann Five, demanded more police action against illegal immigrants and greater powers of detention – and that all immigrants found guilty of a crime be deported. The leader of the far-Right and staunchly anti-immigration Progress Party, Carl Hagen, demanded that all refugees should automatically be considered criminals. Furthermore, society should consider asylum-seekers' 'fitness for freedom' before allowing them out alone on the streets of Norway.[9]

In **Switzerland**, too, a media debate about what to do with 'criminal asylum-seekers' has led the Cabinet to propose a new law that would make it possible to imprison asylum-seekers suspected of a criminal offence and illegal immigrants for up to a year without trial. It would also authorise the judiciary to jail asylum-seekers who stray outside their designated canton. Other proposals put forward by various political parties during this period ranged from the withdrawal of the right of appeal and the creation of special military-style barracks for the internment of criminal asylum-seekers, to their immediate repatriation.[10]

The enemy within

Street robbers, welfare scroungers, shoplifters – hardly, one would have thought, the footsoldiers for a major terrorist onslaught against the heartlands of Europe. But the link made by Trevi between immigrants and terrorism is also a connection made popular by the press, citing police and intelligence sources. **Italy** offers a case in point.

In autumn 1992, the Italian daily, *Il Giornale*, carried a series of speculative stories, based on police briefings, which expressed grave concern about the likelihood of a renewed wave of terrorist attacks in Italy and asserted that poor Third World immigrants were likely recruits for the far-Left. The newspaper's evidence of the links between immigrant organisations and violent Left groups consisted of an anti-racist poster condemning racism and fascism and a statement signed by a cross-section of anti-racist, anti-fascist and Left movements. The articles led to a complaint from MEP Eugenio Melandri who pointed out that it was 'incredible that anti-racists and anti-fascists are being put in the dock', while the activities of the blackshirts were excused. He further commented that the effect of such press stories was 'to criminalise all those who struggle for immigrants' rights'.[11]

In the **UK**, the threat of Third World, overseas-inspired terrorism (not linked so specifically to immigrants and asylum-seekers per se) was the theme of an alarmist feature in the London *Evening Standard* (15.10.92) on 'How world extremists set up havens in London', which quoted 'security experts'' concern that 'expatriates' were using the 'anonymity and freedom' of London for fund-raising for 'terrorist wars' and that 'foreign conflicts' could spill over on to its streets. Again, the article was entirely speculative and provided no concrete evidence to substantiate its claims. Instead, it included a 'Guide to the angry factions who could be your neighbour' – photographs and addresses of the buildings of so-called 'terrorist' organisations operating from the UK, including the PLO and the ANC, a Green organisation called 'Earth First', the Shining Path and the oddly-titled 'British Sikhs', among others.

In **Germany**, where the far-Right press exists alongside the mainstream and influences its concerns, the *Junge Freiheit* (Young Freedom) argues that 'unlimited immigration' is welcomed by the Left, bringing, as it does, a ready supply of 'revolutionaries'.[12] Such views echo those of the German state which, in the face of mounting international criticism over its failure to crack down on nazi violence, has sought to deny the specifically nazi (and thus specifically German) content of that violence by placing it under the banner of 'extremism', which may emanate equally from either Left or Right. The answer to such 'extremism' is the assumption of more power by the state to counter what could, in effect, turn into a civil war, a battle between

Left and Right extremisms. Take, for example, the German government's response to the firebomb attack at Solingen in June 1993, which
claimed the lives of five Turks, all women and girls. Chancellor Kohl
neither attended the funeral nor offered sympathy to the Turkish
community, for which he was bitterly criticised. When Kohl finally did
make a speech on the murders at Solingen, his condemnation was
couched in euphemistic generalisations about 'moral decline'
(*Verrohung*).[13] There was no mention of the need for vigilance, let alone
for a struggle against nazism; instead Kohl condemned all forms of
extremism and violence. (It had already become a political commonplace that if Germans had their violent nationalism, well, so did the
Turks and the Kurds.)* Thus, in a speech which should have concen-
trated on sympathy and justice for the Turkish survivors of German
nationalism, Kohl instead asserted that out of 1.8 million Turks in
Germany, 30,000 were members of extremist organisations.

*   *   *

There seem to be two aspects to the concern over the potential
immigrant terrorist threat: the state's first concern, as implied by
Eugenio Melandri MEP, is over the immigrant response to racism and
discrimination and attempts at self-organisation; its second is to
monitor 'exile' activities which are critical of the regimes they have fled
from. The manner in which these concerns mesh together and reinforce
one another can be seen in developments in **Switzerland**.

One blatant example was the conclusion reached by a government
report on *Extremism in Switzerland*, published in March 1992.
Although the report had been commissioned to investigate the spate of
neo-nazi attacks on refugee hostels, it reported that racist attacks were
on the decline, thus minimising the threat from the far Right. It went
on to list foreigner, exile, refugee and Left anti-imperialist groups as a
major danger to the state and recommended increased state
surveillance of these groups.[14]

Similar state paranoia was evidenced in an extraordinary court case
against three Turkish-Kurdish asylum-seekers.

On 14 January 1991, riot police raided the Berne office of the
socialist Turkish-Kurdish journal, *Mucadele*. The raid led to the initial

---

* In November 1993 the German government outlawed the Kurdish Workers Party
(PKK) and thirty-five 'related bodies'. Previously, state bans had been issued against
four German neo-nazi parties. The French government has followed Germany's lead in
banning two Kurdish groups said to be linked to the PKK.

arrest of twenty-six people, including women and children. At the same time, a series of highly prejudicial articles appeared in the *Blick* newspaper (Switzerland's equivalent to the *Sun*), accusing *Mucadele* of orchestrating crime to fund terrorism and of running an extortion racket. Following the police raid, the Swiss public prosecutor sought to manipulate public opinion further at a specially convened press briefing at which he stated that the police had clear information that *Mucadele* was blackmailing people to give money to Dev Sol (which is linked to the Kurdish Workers' Party) and went on to imply that those arrested were involved in drug-trafficking.

The case did not come to court until December 1992, and then it took place amid the kind of security measures associated with major terrorist trials and after much prejudicial press coverage directed against the five men eventually charged. However, police evidence proved derisory. One police officer, asked where he got his evidence from, replied, 'the newspaper *Schweizerzeit*'; another cited the *Blick*. And when the federal attorney's office was called to give evidence on the ideological and terrorist background of *Mucadele*, a note was sent saying that 'special knowledge of Dev-Sol activists does not exist at our offices'.[15] The judge finally suspended the case and ordered a retrial, at which similar criticisms were made of court procedures.

POLICING A SUSPECT COMMUNITY

Having orchestrated public opinion against a suspect community who, as non-citizens, are without rights and have no redress against arbitrary state power, the pan-European state has set about the business of creating mechanisms to control that community.

These mechanisms are twofold. Control is maintained, first, through the threat of expulsion or extradition (the Expulsion Sub-Group of the Ad Hoc Group on Immigration, now part of the K4 Committee under the Maastricht Treaty, drew up a common policy for the expulsion of foreigners against whom irregularities can be found, and the still unsigned External Frontiers Convention has a formulation for a common EU list of 'undesirable aliens') and, second, internally, through state and bureaucratic surveillance and an aggressive form of 'sus' policing. And in all this, the pan-European state and the individual European states act without regard to any concept of civil liberties, and in the process undermine such conventions and guarantees of human rights as do exist.

Deportation for criminal offences

Criminalising 'immigrant' communities wholesale, in the press and public debate, has, as we have seen, made it easier for politicians to call for new legislation to facilitate the deportation of 'foreigners' found guilty of a criminal offence – all of which accords with the workings of the Expulsion Sub-Group.

There is nothing intrinsically new about the deportation from Europe of 'foreigners' convicted of a criminal offence. In the **UK**, **France** and **Belgium**, immigration lawyers and others have protested against what they see as the unfair principle of 'double punishment', whereby immigrants pay once for a crime with a prison sentence and then, on release, are punished once again when they are served with a deportation order. What is different today, however, is, first, the much wider range of offences deemed punishable with a deportation order and, second, the range of offenders who can be deported.

In relation to the latter, asylum-seekers in Europe with permission to stay on humanitarian grounds (as opposed to full refugee status) are among groups who can be deported back to their country of origin if found guilty of a criminal offence.

In **France**, the new Nationality Code, presently under review by the Constitutional Court, will, if passed, make children born in France of immigrant parents vulnerable to deportation by denying them citizenship rights if they have served prison sentences of six months or more. (This is already the case in **Belgium** and **Germany**.)

In **Denmark**, too, current proposals link possession of a criminal record to denial of citizenship – even for such trivial offences as nonpayment of a parking fine.

But what constitutes an offence worthy of an expulsion order? And where do you deport a young person born and bred in your own country, who may have never even visited the country of his or her parents' birth? For asylum-seekers, too often caught between an intimidating bureaucracy which they cannot comprehend, on the one hand, and a pauperisation process, on the other,* what constitutes a criminal offence worthy of deportation back to a country where you face torture and persecution? For Mr Fadi Ibishi, an asylum-seeker from Kosovo, expelled from **Norway**, it was a 75-day sentence for

---

* In much of Europe, asylum-seekers are denied the right to work, have to subsist on meagre allowances well below poverty levels and are allowed to reside only in special hostels. Elsewhere, in the **UK** for example, a formerly more liberal regime granting access to housing, social security, work, etc, is undercut not only by high levels of unemployment, but by new government regulations designed to restrict social and welfare provision. Under the Asylum and Immigration Appeals Act (1993), asylum-seekers have reduced rights to

threatening behaviour (1990) and an argument over change in a restaurant where he worked (1992). He was last reported to be in a Serbian prison camp.[16]

Furthermore, the threat of expulsion for a criminal offence is a massive deterrent to any political organisation against racism and fascism and for civil rights among the disenfranchised. Politicians are well aware of this. For instance, in **France**, after disturbances in Paris following the death in police custody of a Zairean youth, Makone M'Bowle, in April 1993, minister of the interior Charles Pasqua announced that, in future, 'foreigners caught on demonstrations resulting in damage to property and looting will be liable to expulsion orders'.[17]

In **Italy**, present attempts to widen the deportation net to include immigrants committed for trial, or simply remanded in custody on suspicion of having committed offences such as arson, damage to property, theft or receipt of stolen property, are being resisted by immigrant and civil liberties organisations and the newly-formed Association for Democratic Lawyers. It had been proposed, under Article 8 of the Conso decree, that an immigrant arrested for the above offences could be deported even before standing trial. Minister of justice Conso has defended himself against allegations of racism by saying that the decree will apply to any foreigner and not just to non-EU citizens. He also claims that the deportation of immigrants without any hearing is in their own interests and will not occur without the consent of the deportee. Yet, in practice, even this apparent concession does not seem to be made, as was demonstrated by the case of Mohamed Firuzi, a self-employed Iranian architect who has lived in Palermo, Sicily, for ten years and has three children and an Italian wife.

When Mr Firuzi went to the police station to apply for a residence permit, he was refused. He protested angrily and the head of the 'foreigners section' of the police was called; he produced a file on Mr Firuzi, including details of a criminal record. (Three years before, Mr Firuzi had received a three-month suspended sentence for being in possession of three grams of cannabis.) The officer, on finding this out, issued Mr Firuzi with a deportation order and told him: 'As far as

---

housing as homeless persons. While awaiting a decision on their application, asylum-seekers receive only 90 per cent of basic income support. DSS offices routinely ask to see an asylum-seeker's Standard Acknowledgment Letter or SAL (a document on passport paper bearing the holder's photograph, name, date of birth and nationality) before issuing benefits. As it can take several months to obtain the document, thousands of asylum-seekers are unable to obtain benefit and are rendered destitute.

I am concerned, with this on your record, you're already out of the country. And you can take your family with you.'

Mr Firuzi has now lost his appeal against the deportation order. Another appeal is pending.[18]

Deportation on national security grounds

Also caught in the 'deportation net' are those accused of aiding terrorism or whose presence is deemed inimical to the 'national security' of the host states. Somewhat outside the timescale of this report, but nonetheless indicative of the coming trend, were the Europe-wide deportations of Arabs – many of them residents of long standing – during the Gulf war. Again, the 'evidence' of the threat they posed to national security was withheld from the accused. (A number of the deportees were themselves political opponents of dictatorial Arab regimes who would have been at risk on their return.)

What constitutes 'national security' is defined in ever widening terms. In **Sweden**, two Palestinians were deported after a special court pronounced them members of Abu Nidal. They had no right to see the evidence against them.[19]

In its use of the 'national security' argument, the **UK**, which refuses to ratify Protocol 4 of the European Human Rights Convention (ensuring freedom of movement and settlement within one's own country), may have something to teach its European neighbours. The case of John Matthews, a 22-year-old postgraduate from Belfast, has highlighted the British practice of imposing internal exile through orders made under the Prevention of Terrorism Act of 1989. This, like its predecessors, allows for a person to be excluded from the UK as a whole, from Britain only, or from Northern Ireland only. In July 1993, after a case in which Mr Matthews had been brought to court on an explosives charge but where no evidence had been offered against him, he was immediately rearrested. The magistrate had said that he would leave the court without a stain on his character; but the Home Secretary then saw fit to serve him with an exclusion order, on the grounds of national security.[20]

In **Belgium**, the new Tobback law, which provides for accelerated procedures for political asylum, contains provisions allowing for the detention of asylum-seekers and other foreigners considered by the minister of the interior to be a danger to public order or national security.

By such means, conventions and laws which state that no refugees with a well-founded fear of persecution should be returned to their countries of origin are being steadily whittled away. Another pressing issue for those concerned with the future of democracy in Europe is the proposed change to long-established European conventions on extradition. In justifying its plans to include offences of a political nature in the list of extraditable offences, the EC justice ministers, meeting in Limelette in September 1993, argued that, as all EC states respect human rights and are democratic, there are no longer any grounds for refusing extradition requests. In practice, in the **UK** and **Spain**, the blanket suspicion cast over the Irish and Basque communities as 'terrorist', and the kind of human rights abuses this engenders, has spilt over into the policing of immigrant communities. Amnesty International has, for instance, highlighted the use of torture on Basques suspected of collaboration with ETA (including the use of simulated executions, electric shocks, and plastic bags being placed over the suspect's head). It has also alleged that torture was used against two Moroccans by members of the Civil Guard in Ibiza in 1992.

Furthermore, some European countries seem to be entering into new extradition arrangements,* sometimes formal, sometimes informal, with various countries outside the EC, and the evidence points to geopolitical and economic concerns, not human rights, as the motivating factor. The **UK** has ratified an extradition treaty with India which removes the possibility of a political defence in extradition proceedings. The *Times* commented matter-of-factly that 'the accord is another sign of the increasing involvement between the two countries following the collapse of the Soviet Union, India's main ally, and Delhi's decision to open its economy to foreign investors. The British government believes India offers vast potential for investment.'[21]

Belgium may not have formalised its links with India via such a treaty, but, in an extraordinary case in October 1993, the authorities arrested Amanullah Khan, the chairman of the Jammu Kashmir Liberation Front, who had travelled from Pakistan (where he has lived for fifteen years) to Brussels with a valid visa issued by the Belgian embassy in Pakistan. He was to address a meeting of the Socialist Group of the European Parliament (GPES). The Belgian authorities say the arrest followed a tip-off from Interpol that Mr Khan was wanted in India on charges of murder. But, as William Claes, the foreign affairs spokesperson for the GPES, asked, why did the Belgian government provide Mr Khan with a visa to attend the conference, despite protests from India, simply in order to subject him to an extra-

---

* See 'Exporting immigration control' (p27).

dition procedure? The whole affair smacks of entrapment in which the European Parliament and Belgium are unhappily implicated.[22]

Whereas in cases of political extradition the state has had to announce its case against the accused (even as it withholds its evidence), other categories of expulsion are taking place even more surreptitiously. In exchange for beneficial trade agreements, financial aid, etc, a number of countries on the southern and eastern fringe of Europe appear to be cooperating with the deportation and expulsion of their own nationals from the EU.

Germany and **Romania**, however, have signed a formal agreement. In this case, Germany deports asylum-seekers back to Romania, which accepts them in exchange for monetary assistance to the Romanian government. Nearly one-third of the 3,000 refugees deported from Berlin to Bucharest by March 1993 were Romanies, who face undoubted and persistent persecution in the country. They were sent back under the escort of members of the Romanian security forces.[23] Following Germany's lead, the French interior minister, Charles Pasqua, has suggested that **France** should enter into an arrangement with **Romania** whereby, in exchange for providing resettlement grants via the French consulate in Bucharest, Romanian Gypsies in France are repatriated.[24] In fact, a repatriation programme of Romanian Gypsies camped in Nanterre in the western suburbs of Paris commenced in January 1994.

At present, Association Agreements have been entered into between the EU and Turkey, Morocco, Algeria and Tunisia, as well as Hungary, Romania, the Czech and Slovak Republics, Bulgaria and Poland. In parallel with these agreements, arrangements are springing up – formal and informal – which enable EU countries to deport foreign nationals from 'associated' countries, often on the flimsiest of pretexts. And the very existence of such cooperation assumes that the participating countries are themselves 'safe' for their own political dissidents.

Among the more disturbing cases that have come to light is that of Abdennacer Ben Yussef, a Tunisian metalworker who had lived in **Italy** with his wife and children for a number of years. He disappeared without trace after he had visited the local police station to renew his residence permit. When his pregnant wife went to the station to find out where he was, she was held and questioned, but was told nothing. Weeks later, she found out that her husband – who had no criminal record and had never been a member of any Tunisian opposition group (he was a member of the perfectly legal Union of Tunisian Immigrant

Workers) – had been expelled from Italy to Tunisia (where he was imprisoned and tortured). He has since escaped. The Italian government says the expulsion was carried out on grounds of 'national security'. He had, in effect, been kidnapped by the authorities and expelled with no regard to the due process of law.[25]

Again, when Tunisian W Bennani arrived in **Belgium** claiming political asylum, his application was initially refused unseen at the airport because of the intervention of Tunisian police. This was in line with a Belgo-Tunisian convention on mutual juridical assistance. Later, a decision in the Conseil d'État, Belgium's highest legal body, resulted in an expulsion order being revoked.[26]

Similar agreements with Algeria could, it is believed, have precipitated a number of arrests in **France** and **Germany** of leading exiled members of the Islamic Salvation Front (FIS). In Paris, police swoops on the homes of FIS members in November 1993 were justified by the government as a response to the recent abduction of French consular officials in Algiers and to prevent political acts of violence on French soil. But even the staunchly conservative *Le Figaro* described the link established by the police between the two as 'tenuous'.[27] The lawyer for Nastreddine El Hamdi, a former member of the dissolved Islamic parliament now living in France, has described a deportation order against him as 'disguised extradition', and points out that his client would agree to go to any other country but Algeria.[28] And in **Germany**, there is concern that the unexplained arrest of Rabah Kabir, a spokesman-in-exile for Algeria's Islamic Front, was prompted by the new cooperation between the German and Algerian governments. Kabir is currently under sentence of death imposed by the Algerian authorities.[29]

That such agreements should, *de facto*, override internationally accepted conventions on human rights makes a mockery of international guarantees of the right to asylum. Will the list of 'safe countries' being drawn up in secret by the successors to the Ad-Hoc Group on Immigration further degrade international standards on the right to asylum?

Police powers and police methods

The way in which immigrants are stereotyped and suspected as illegals, criminals and terrorists in the media helps to create the climate for the granting of special powers to the police. And such policing is aimed not at the individual 'suspect' but at the immigrant communities as a whole. It takes the form of computerised databases on immigrant communities, the saturation policing of immigrant areas, mass identity checks and police raids on immigrant meeting places, cafés, etc. Such policing, which stereotypes immigrants collectively as criminals, legitimises popular racism.

In **Norway**, it recently emerged that the police had been breaking the terms of the Norwegian computerised foreigners' register. The FREMKON register allows the police to record information, in a secret code, on the criminal records of foreigners. But the police had also used this facility to record information on foreigners merely suspected of crime.[30]

As Giuliano Campioni, a professor at the University of Pisa and president of Africa-Insieme, put it after a brutal racist attack on an immigrant leader in Rome, **Italy**, 'It is time now to say no to the criminalisation of immigrants. Every morning in our area, police vans arrive hunting for illegal immigrants. Such police operations reinforce images of immigrants as criminals and heighten racism.'[31]

Many of the police forces in Europe look to the British police as providing a model for the policing of immigrant communities, particularly 'unassimilable' second-generation youth. The saturation-style policing of black areas, the wide-scale random stops of black individuals, the existence of specialist squads like the Territorial Support Group to police the **UK**'s black communities (which are all redolent of the 'occupying force' of a colonial police) are becoming more common throughout Europe's major cities. The infamous UK 'sus' law, under which a person could be arrested simply on the suspicion that he or she was about to commit an offence, was abolished in 1981 but was replaced by a more sophisticated and intensive style of paramilitary policing within the framework of special powers granted by the Police and Criminal Evidence Act 1984 and Public Order Act 1986. These supplemented those already in existence under the Prevention of Terrorism Act.

Belgium and the **Netherlands**, it would seem, are following the current British pattern of granting the police special powers. In **Belgium**, for instance, special 'security operations' are, as of 1993, being mounted in eight districts of Brussels where 'immigrant' youth are said to gather 'in hostility to the forces of law and order'.[32] In **France**, policing methods seem to echo the earlier pattern of British police racism typified by the 'sus' laws.

Hence, the new French nationality legislation includes a specific 'Bill on the Reinforcement of Identity Checks' which allows police to stop and search someone on the suspicion that he or she is a foreigner.

The official wording of the Bill, which is being challenged by the constitutional court, specifies that the police can carry out identity checks based on 'any element other than membership of a racial group' that allows the officer to presume someone is a 'foreigner'. Evidence to justify such a check could be as slight as the possession of a newspaper in a foreign language.

But who will the police suspect of being a 'foreigner'? It is precisely someone's colour that marks him or her out to the police as potentially 'illegal'. And when the police define any non-white persons as suspected illegal immigrants, merely by virtue of skin colour, then their arrest – carried out with force if necessary – is seen as justified, whether or not any crime has been committed.

Thus, in **Belgium**, in early 1993, an Algerian man phoned the local Brussels police to report a minor car accident. When the police arrived, they immediately asked to see the man's identity papers. After an argument, during which the man phoned the national gendarmerie to complain about the attitude of the local officers, police reinforcements arrived and, it is alleged, handcuffed the Algerian man and threw him into the back of a police van, where they beat him. So severe were his injuries that he was taken by the police to hospital where they told the doctor that the Algerian had been in a car accident.[33]

Previously, in February 1992, in Schaerbeek, a Brussels suburb, three plainclothes police officers had approached Mohammed J, a petrol station attendant of Pakistani origin, and asked to see his identity papers. When Mr J had been unable to produce them immediately, they had assaulted him.[34] Another man, a 19-year-old immigrant, is suing the police following an incident in which he suffered brain damage. The incident began when the police asked him to put out his cigarette on the underground. When he went to leave, saying he would finish his cigarette outside, they asked to see his identity card. The man alleges he was then handcuffed and beaten with a police baton.[35]

In **Spain**, in March 1992, 25-year-old Moroccan Hamid Raaji was stopped by an officer in Valencia and asked to produce his papers. When Mr Raaji protested, saying, 'I'm not in the Third World, I'm in Spain', he was beaten by the policeman, who kneed him in the groin while three other police officers stood by and watched. The attack resulted in the Moroccan having surgery to remove one of his testicles.[36]

SOS Racism in Valencia, who took up Mr Raaji's case, described it as one of the worst racist attacks ever to have taken place in the province. Another case, taken up by SOS Racism's Barcelona branch, involved a Nigerian man who, in April 1992, was violently beaten up by the police, who dragged him out of a phone booth on the grounds that they suspected him of being in possession of drugs.[37]

⚸ As these cases show, 'sus' policing leads to excessive violence on the part of police officers. It can also lead to the police dealing out a frightening and deadly form of summary justice.

In **France**, Makone M'Bowle, a 17-year-old Zairean, was arrested in Paris during a mass swoop, accompanied by identity checks, on the Goutte d'Or district in April 1993. At the police station, he was shot in the head by the officer interrogating him. The officer, who has been charged with manslaughter, said that he was only trying to frighten the youth into making a confession. Around the same time, Rachid Ardjouni, a 17-year-old Arab immigrant, died after being shot in the head by police in Wattrelos, northern France. Ardjouni was supposed to have been seen trespassing on school grounds. These are only the latest in a long catalogue of deaths of young immigrants in France, many of which have sparked off angry confrontations with the police.[38]

This kind of summary justice is not confined to France or Belgium (where, in 1992 alone, four 'immigrant' youth died in police custody). In **Portugal**, in January 1992, an Angolan was shot dead by a police officer in Damaia, a Lisbon suburb, when he refused to get into a police car after being stopped and asked to produce his identity papers.[39] And in **Germany**, in 1992, a Romanian refugee, Lorin Ladu, was shot and killed in a police station in Stassfurt, Sachsen-Anhalt, allegedly while trying to escape.[40] In September 1993, another Romanian refugee, aged 24, was shot and seriously injured in a police station in Waldhaus, near the German/Czech border. The shooting, it is alleged, happened when he refused to show his identity papers to the police.[41]

Such cases have to be seen, not as isolated examples, but as part of a general trend across Europe, in which the lowest common denominators of each country's policing practices are being universalised, and against a background in which the standard of treatment of those in police custody gives cause for concern.* In southern Europe, for example, concerted police raids to hunt out 'illegals' are a relatively new phenomenon and a direct result of the single European market and the removal of borders. Previously, in Spain and Italy, undocumented workers were considered a necessary and tolerated part of the national economy which, in certain sectors, relied heavily on seasonal

---

* In **France**, the Council of Europe's Commission on the Prevention of Torture points to the 'not inconsiderable risk' to suspects of 'being mistreated whilst in police detention'. And the torture of suspected ETA members in Spain has already been cited.

and temporary workers. It is not hard to see that the policing of 'immigrant' communities in this way (itself brought in to satisfy their other European partners of southern Europe's 'firmness' on immigration controls), when combined with long-standing traditions of police violence – the residue of long periods of dictatorship – makes for an explosive mix of racism and authoritarianism.

SUSPECTING THE VICTIMS

If the upsurge in racism and fascism across Europe is not placed in its proper context of state and popular racism, it is inevitable that a 'blaming the victim' syndrome emerges. As each country has brought in asylum and immigration legislation, in accordance with the dictates of pan-European racism, politicians have sought to debate the refugee issue in terms of numbers and not of need. Standard clichés are that 'the boat is full' or we have reached 'the threshold of tolerance'; refugees are labelled as economic migrants and 'Euro-scroungers'.

In fact, 'the boat is full' was originally the slogan of the far-Right Republikaner Party in Germany; now it is used by all German mainstream political parties. In September 1991, just eight days before the pogrom at Hoyerswerda, the right-wing popular magazine, *Der Spiegel*, blazoned the slogan on its front cover, complete with an illustration depicting Germany as a massively overcrowded boat, surrounded by a sea of struggling humanity, with a sub-title 'The onslaught of the poor'.[42]

Just as the argument in the 1960s and 1970s in the UK was that 'fewer numbers make for better race relations' (ie, the presence of black people was the cause of race conflict), the argument today is that 'fewer refugees make for less fascism' – which, taken to its logical conclusion, as Sivanandan points out, means 'no refugees, no fascism' – and that is not a far cry from the 'final solution'.[43]

This is not to say that the governments of Europe are not concerned to curtail the rise of racism and fascism – neo-nazi parties are, if nothing else, a threat to law and order and disruptive of the political status quo. However, at the same time as clamping down on fascist organisations, the state uses the violence that the fascists engender to justify calls for legislative change to tighten refugee and immigration procedure. Thus, by being seen to be in agreement with the far-Right claim that immigration is the root cause of Europe's social problems, the state fuels the nazi violence further, and no more so than in **Germany**. Here, a sustained political campaign to remove Article 16 from the German constitution, which guaranteed the right to political asylum, immediately followed the events of Rostock in August 1992. Here, 100 Vietnamese men, women and children were snatched from almost certain death after nazis had set fire to a refugee hostel which adjoined the guestworkers' premises. Barely had the flames died down, than Social Democrats found common cause with Christian Democrats in calling for the abolition of Germany's constitutional right to asylum and tougher immigration laws to stop 'illegal immigrants' and 'fake asylum-seekers'. And the MP for Mecklenburg furthered the hysteria by arguing that it had become impossible for the people of Rostock to tolerate the 200 asylum-seekers who were crowded into a small area.[44]

But the link made between the numbers of asylum-seekers and immigrants and the rise in racism and fascism is not confined to Germany. In 1991, the **UK** prime minister, John Major, told the Luxembourg Summit that 'if we fail in our control efforts we risk fuelling the far Right'. The mayor of Villa Literno, **Italy**, reacted to a 3,000-strong demonstration against immigrant seasonal workers in July 1993 by arguing that 'the village can't tolerate another invasion'.[45] The mayor of St Truiden, in northern **Belgium**, sought to put the blame for a firebomb attack on a house occupied by twenty-five Sikhs on the high number of Sikhs working in the region for the fruit harvest. He had refused to register them at the town hall.[46] And in **Austria**, after an attack on a refugee centre in Gutenstein, near Vienna, in September 1992, the mayors of Salzburg and Vienna responded to the outrage by announcing that they would take in no more refugees. Fascist violence was appeased, not condemned.

Identifying with the perpetrator
As a suspect community, the 'immigrants' have no civil liberties. And this lack of rights is also reflected in the failure to afford them protection from attack. Indeed, as their presence is seen as the cause of increased racism and fascism, they are held responsible for bringing the violence upon themselves and for causing dislocation and social problems throughout European society.

What is of concern here is not so much the police's response to individual racist attacks as the mounting evidence to suggest that immigrants and refugees are considered outside the protection of the law. In the many instances of what can only be described as orchestrated racist campaigns against immigrants, the manner in which the police abrogate any responsibility demonstrates an underlying sympathy with the perpetrators and contempt for the victims. Thus, the government of the **Netherlands** was recently criticised by the UN Committee for the Elimination of All Forms of Racial Discrimination for failing to enforce its criminal laws against racism. The ruling concerned the case of LK, a partially-disabled Moroccan citizen, who, in August 1989, was met by a reception committee of local racists when he went to view a house offered to him by the council. They threatened to burn the house down and damage his car if he moved in, but the police refused to prosecute.[47]

In **Germany**, a parliamentary committee investigating the events of Rostock discovered the existence of a verbal agreement between the head of police operations and the racist and fascist mob. In evidence to the committee, police inspector Waldemar Skrocki stated that his men wanted to intervene to prevent the attacks on refugee centres in Mecklenburg but were stopped by the head of police operations. His instruction to the men to 'pull back for half an hour' left the mob free to set fire to the refugee hostel, almost killing 100 Vietnamese men, woman and children who lived next door.[48]

It is not just police who demonstrate such contempt: local municipal authorities, with an eye to their voters, also connive at the hounding and expulsion of immigrant and seasonally migrant communities who are forced to exist on the margins of society. Often homeless and poverty-stricken, they set up makeshift camps on the outskirts of the city. They are regarded as a social eyesore, to be removed at all costs. And in the collusion by the authorities in local campaigns to force them out can also be seen strong parallels with the experience of Europe's Romanies, victims of prejudice for centuries. Nowhere is this seen more clearly than in **Italy**, where mob violence against immigrant and seasonal migrant workers in 1993 reached frightening proportions.

Towards the end of May 1993, a series of arson attacks were carried out against the Borghetto Prenestino, a ghetto on the outskirts of Rome, where 1,000 homeless north African families lived. In one incident, 100 immigrants were left homeless when forty barracks were set ablaze. In another incident, twelve nazis sought to enter the camp, armed with batons and petrol bombs, but were repelled by the immigrants. Although the nazis were allegedly stopped by the police, they were simply released without their names and addresses being taken.

The protests against the immigrants had been led by the Quarticciola neighbourhood committee. On 6 May, 400 people, including known fascists, protested in front of the local town hall, asking for the neighbourhood to be cleared of 'thieves, drug dealers and drunkards'. During the demonstration, the police announced that the camp would be demolished on 10 May. When the demolition was delayed, the fire and other attacks cited above took place.

On 31 May, the camp was levelled to make way for a major commercial venture. A small number of the homeless were moved to the outskirts of Rome, but the majority were left to live on the road and the fields of Quarticciola, vulnerable to further racist attacks.[49]

The police and local municipality response to what has been described as a 'black hunt', during which 500 migrant workers were forced to flee from the south-eastern region of Puglia in September 1993, seems to have been to apportion blame equally between migrants and Italians. Whereas twenty Italians, most of them agricultural labourers, were arrested in Stornara and accused of leading the violence, police rounded up 150 Algerians, Moroccans and Tunisians and packed them into trains and coaches and sent them off to Naples, several hours' journey away. A local Christian Democrat politician, commenting on the violence, called for a revision of the Martelli law on the grounds that the worsening economic and employment crisis and 'disorderly flow' of non-EC citizens 'runs the risk of sparking an explosion in our country'. The Socialist deputy mayor's response to the violence was to say that 'nothing special has happened'.[50]

In **Spain**, a group of fifty seasonal workers from the Maghreb, who went on strike in August 1993 to expose the racism they had suffered, were accused by the mayor of the village of Massalcoreig, Lerida, of setting fire to their own shelter and stealing from local people. The 200 migrant workers, mostly from Morocco and Algeria, came to the village for the harvest. They were given no lodgings, and most slept in the open fields. Some found a deserted pigsty and erected temporary shelters there, but these were burnt out by locals. The migrant workers accused the mayor of refusing to take action to protect them, instead regularly harassing them and demanding to see their identity papers.[51]

In **France**, on 29 October 1992, 1,000 gendarmes, including members of the CRS (riot police), forcibly evicted 312 homeless black families from the Vincennes camp, on the outskirts of Paris. Before the evictions, the Front National had carried out at least three demonstrations against the camp. Ten days before the police-led eviction, 200 FN members protested outside the Ministry of Towns chanting slogans such as 'Housing for the French' and 'We've had enough of Arabs and Negroes'.[52]

Again in France, after the mayor of Nanterre (a suburb to the north of Paris) had announced that 150 Romanies residing there would be 'transferred' to Neuville-sur-Ain, 500 kms away in eastern France, Neuville's residents launched a campaign so vociferous that the mayor was forced to abandon the plan. Residents organised themselves into brigades and armed themselves with clubs, knives and old tyres, and proclaimed themselves prepared to do anything to stop the Gypsies coming to town. The local mayor, Joseph Perrot, joined in the protests, declaring on *France 2 TV* that 'We have to block the roads and warn other towns' in order 'to prevent the invasion'. During protests, residents carried banners with slogans such as 'We do not want this rubbish', 'Out with the invaders' and 'Send them back to their own country'.[53]

In **Germany**, villagers from Eichof, in Mecklenburg-Vorpommern, organised a blockade to keep asylum-seekers out of their community. When three buses with 156 refugees arrived at a camp close to the village, a mob forced them back. But, instead of punishing the attackers, the regional interior ministry decided to disperse the refugees to other places.[54]

Such popular campaigns, against the vulnerable and the homeless or those just deemed different, are terrifying in their potential to arouse mob violence and hysteria. And to deny – at the level of government, of the state – that such attacks are racially motivated serves only to confirm this burning hatred as reasonable and legitimate. This is nowhere more obvious than in the attitude of the authorities to the Romany in the countries of the former eastern European bloc. In **Hungary**, the minister of the interior could discover no racial motivation in a pogrom against Romanies that took place in the village of Ketegyhaza on the great Hungarian plain.[55] Villagers threw petrol bombs into the windows of Gypsy homes and burnt their horses alive in the stables. In the **Czech Republic** there was no official comment after the brutal killing of four Romanies in the space of one week in September 1993.[56]

Incidents such as the pogrom at Ketegyhaza might be expected to rouse in the 'majority' a sense of shame that an ugly racism should rear its head in this brutal manner. For such shame to manifest itself, there must be some sympathy, some identification with the victims, as fellow human beings. But just as Romanies are seen as outsiders, so too are 'foreigners' deemed outside the reckoning of justice. Black victims of racist attacks are not taken seriously, they do not count; they are here on sufferance and should be prepared to tolerate whatever happens to them. For example, in **Switzerland**, arson attacks in 1992 and 1993 against refugee centres have been dismissed as the work of drunken hooligans, and so are not considered to reflect any greater malaise in Swiss society.

One exception, however, was the report of a Swiss parliamentary committee on racism and xenophobia, which detailed 400 incidents of right-wing motivated racist activity that occurred between April 1985 and March 1993. The report criticised the response of the police and the judiciary to racial harassment; its author says that the victims of violence 'are not taken seriously at the police station, but are laughed at, or simply got rid of'. In one documented incident, concerning an attack on a Tamil man during a demonstration in Bern on 27 February 1993, the perpetrator, it seems, escaped from the scene in a police car. 'Just accidental', said a police spokesperson in reply to criticisms.[57]

Proving innocence

Often it is suggested, without any apparent evidence, that the victims of the attacks are themselves criminals – thus serving to reinforce the notion of immigrants as a criminal community, to deny the relevance of racial violence and allow the perpetrators to escape serious penalties.

In **Italy**, two Moroccans were waiting at traffic lights for a chance to wash car windows when two men drew up on a large motor bike and one opened fire with a machine gun. Elrain Ermahumuni, aged 29, was shot in the foot; the other man was shot in the arm and the abdomen. His identity was not made public and doctors refused to say how long it would take him to recover.

According to *Il Manifesto* (10.2.93), there have been three similar cases in the same area. In at least two of these cases, the attackers were young locals, who regard 'foreigners' as invading their 'territory'. Although the police were aware of the identity of the youths, their only action has been to advise 'foreigners' living in the same area to avoid certain streets.

In the case of the Moroccan men, the police have, it seems, closed the case with undue haste, failing to identify the attackers. Their suggestion that the Moroccan men were drug pushers, and that this was little more than an underworld shooting, has been reproduced in local papers. *Il Giornale*, for example, labelled the shooting an underground 'score settling' – though why putative drug dealers should have to wash car windows to make ends meet is not explained. The result is that it is the Moroccans who must prove their innocence.

In many other instances, the first response of the police is to ask to see the immigrants' identity papers, as happened to two Senegalese men who went to the police in June 1993. They wanted to report a vicious attack during which a friend had been thrown from a first-floor window by an Italian gang armed with knives and a stick. An Italian friend of the Senegalese men was told by a police officer: 'There's no point overdoing it. We know what foreigners are like. Often they don't even speak Italian very well.' [58]

In **France**, in February 1989, Maria-Jose Garnier shot dead Ali Rafa after he allegedly attempted to steal a croissant from her bakery in Reims. When the case finally came to court in 1992, Garnier's lawyer, a member of the organisation 'Légitime Défense', presented the killing as a case of self-defence, and the judge ruled out racism as a contributory factor. Considerable evidence emerged, however, to suggest that Ms Garnier had often refused to serve Maghrebians and that she and her husband used weapons in an 'ostentatious' way. When Garnier was acquitted, the lawyer for Ali Rafa's family commented, 'The life of a man is worth less than a croissant.'[59]

In **Germany**, in 1992, the murderer of a Vietnamese guestworker was given a four-and-a-half year sentence for manslaughter. Nguyen Van Tu had been stabbed to death on the streets of Berlin-Marzahn in April 1992. The murderer, who admitted in court to being a member of the neo-nazi Deutsche Volksunion, said that he had killed the man because he had been selling contraband cigarettes. The judge ruled that the killing had nothing to do with hatred of foreigners but was a case of 'reprehensible arbitrary law'.[60]

Furthermore, all too often, any attempt at self-defence is interpreted as making trouble and provoking 'indigenous' youth.

In **Finland**, a fight between ten Finnish and ten Somali youth in Joensuu in February 1993 led to the prosecution of one person: a Somali who allegedly used a knife during the fight and was jailed for one year. During the court case, it emerged that Somalis had been regularly threatened and abused in Joensuu, and the Somali who was finally convicted had been threatened in his home. During the trial, a group of fifteen Finns gathered in the courtroom. When the Somali youth attempted to give his statement, the Finns started shouting in an attempt to drown him out.[61]

The singling out of one Somali for police prosecution identifies him as the troublemaker. The young Finns, on the other hand, are treated as having legitimate grievances: it is understandable if they direct their frustrations towards the Somalis. Such an approach, which turns the aggressors into objects of sympathy in need of social understanding, while the victims of attack are turned into criminals if they fight back, has been taken to the extreme in **Germany** where projects to rehabilitate skinhead youth and provide sensitivity training for neo-nazis have been set up, accompanied by (now discredited) fact-finding trips to Israel and Turkey. In **Hungary**, where the minister of the interior described most skinheads as 'honest Hungarians' and where a member of the ruling Democratic Forum described neo-nazis petitioning parliament as 'well-intentioned children', this tendency exists too.[62]

Where, in all of this, is society's identification with the oppressed? What message does the state offer to the victim of racist and fascist violence? Politicians concentrate not on the duty of the state to protect, but on the duty the victim owes society not to resist, not to fight back. Not once, in the recent history of racist and fascist murders in Europe, has a leading government politician visited a bereaved immigrant family to express sympathy or offer promise of justice. Indeed, Chancellor Kohl's eventual statement on the Solingen murders added insult to injury when he warned foreigners that they would be deported if they used violence in reaction to this horrendous crime.[63]

And then, who are the foreigners? Although many of these settlers may have lived in Europe for long periods and their children been born here, they are still often deemed 'immigrants', as are their children. For the route to citizenship by birth (*ius soli*, or right of soil) has been gradually narrowing throughout the post-war period in favour of a citizenship by descent (*ius sanguinis*, or right of blood). Of the Turkish community in Germany, it has been estimated that over 70 per cent are the children of Turkish immigrants born on German soil. If it were not for Germany's citizenship laws, based on blood, these 'foreigners' would be seen for what they are – German citizens of Turkish descent. These German/Turkish citizens are being attacked by German nazis, yet the German state says it will deport the German/Turks for fighting back!

Without citizenship rights, second- and third-generation youth, forever immigrants, can only fight racism with both hands tied behind their backs. Citizenship rights would untie their hands and undermine the edifice of racism and fascism, the ideology of suspicion and stigmatisation, upon which the new Fortress Europe is built.

References
1   See special issue of *Race & Class*, 'Europe: variations on a theme of racism' (Vol 32, no 3, January-March 1991).
2   *Migration Newssheet* October and November 1993.

3   See Mieke Hopper, 'Letter from the Netherlands', *CARF* No 8, May/June 1992.
4   *Het Parool* 3.11.92.
5   *Volkskrant* 1.2.93.
6   *Jyllands Posten* 1, 29, 30, 31.10.92.
7   *Ibid* 27.6.93.
8   *Ibid* 9, 30.6.93.
9   *Samora Newsletter* March, April 1993.
10 *Le Nouveau Quotidien* 31.7.93, 30.8.93, 6, 24, 28.9.93; *Le Courrier* 16, 23.8.93, 4, 5, 24.9.93.
11 *Il Manifesto* 31.10.92.
12 See Teun A van Dijk, 'The press and racism in Germany and Europe', International Association for the Study of Racism, University of Amsterdam, June 1993.
13 *Ibid.*
14 Analysis of the report provided by the 'Komitee Schluss mit dem Schnüffelstaat'.
15 *Weltwoche* 18.2.93.
16 *Samora Newsletter* March 1993.
17 *Migration Newssheet* May 1993.
18 *Il Manifesto* 1.7.93.
19 *Eskilstuna* 11.12.92, as cited in *Migration Newssheet* January 1993.
20 *Times* 7.7.93.
21 16.11.93.
22 *Eastern Eye* 16.11.93.
23 *Die Tageszeitung* 15.1.93.
24 *Liberation* 1.9.93.
25 See *CARF* No 14, May/June 1993. The case of Abdennacer Ben Yussef has been taken up by the Italian civil liberties group, Senza Confine, and by Amnesty International.
26 *Migration Newssheet* August 1992.
27 As cited in *Weekly Journal* 18.11.93.
28 *Liberation* 10.5.93.
29 *Al-Muhajir* 15.6.93.
30 *Samora Newsletter* August 1993.
31 *Il Manifesto* 20.3.93.
32 *Solidaire* No 26, 23.6.93.
33 *Ibid* 2.2.93.
34 The officers involved were subsequently sentenced to six months' imprisonment. See *Solidaire* 16.12.92.
35 *Solidaire* 15.9.93.
36 *El Pais* 15.3.92.
37 Four officers were subsequently arrested and sentenced to ten days' imprisonment for the assault: see *El Pais* 3.3.92.
38 *Guardian* 15.4.93; *Newsweek* 19.4.93.
39 *Expresso* 31.1.92.
40 *Die Tageszeitung* 22.1.93.
41 *Taz* 23.9.93.
42 Peter Jensen, '*Der Spiegel:* racial nationalism goes mainstream in a German newsweekly', in *FAIR* July/August 1992.
43 A. Sivanandan, 'Racism: the road from Germany', in *Race & Class*, Vol 34, no 3, January-March 1993.
44 See *CARF* No 10 September-October 1992.
45 *Il Manifesto* 30.7.93.
46 *Independent* 18.8.93; *IPS* 20.8.93.
47 *Human Rights Law Journal* Vol 14, nos 7-8, 30.9.93.
48 As reported in *Die Tageszeitung* 10.3.93.

49   *Il Manifesto* 16.7.93.
50   *Il Manifesto* 18, 20, 24, 28.9.93.
51   *El Periodico* 4, 5.8.93.
52   *Liberation* 20.10.92; *Guardian* 30.10.92, 2.11.92; *CARF* November/December 1992.
53   *Inter-Press Service News* 8.3.92.
54   *Die Tageszeitung* 26.3.93.
55   *Independent on Sunday* 25.10.92.
56   See Bella Edginton, 'To kill a Romany', *Race & Class* Vol 35, no 3, January-March 1994.
57   *Bund* 23.4.93.
58   *Il Manifesto* 20.6.93.
59   *L'Humanité* 12, 13, 14.11.92.
60   *Die Tageszeitung* 9.10.92.
61   *Karjalainen* 16.4.93.
62   *Le Monde* 28.11.92; *Magyar Hirlap* 2.2.93.
63   As cited in *Migration Newssheet* July 1993.

2 Exporting immigration control

The governments of western Europe have, in recent years, become ever more brutally and blatantly efficient in deterring and removing immigrants and asylum-seekers. Increasingly harsh measures, agreed at European and implemented at national level, are justified by the equation of the concepts 'refugee', 'illegal immigrant', 'criminal' and 'threat to public order': or, in other words, by the criminalisation and dehumanisation of immigrants and refugees. In relation to refugees, this process has enabled European states to get round the provisions of the Geneva Convention[1] while simultaneously claiming (although ever less convincingly) to uphold it. More importantly, it has meant shifting the asylum-seekers – and the refugee 'problem' – out of their territory altogether.

In this project, they have involved the central and eastern European states and, to a lesser extent, the countries of the Maghreb, forcing those countries to become western Europe's first line of immigration control: its *cordon sanitaire*.

Building the perimeter fence

Since the mid-1980s, when the 'harmonisation' of western European immigration and refugee control got under way, the aim was to create an impregnable outer border round the EU, since the abolition of internal frontiers envisaged by the Single European Act would mean that, once 'they had breached the perimeter fence, *terrorists, drug-smugglers, other criminals, refugees and other undesirables* would be able to circulate freely'[2] (in the words of the House of Lords Select Committee). [our emphasis]

Securing the fences around western Europe's perimeter was thus the order of the day in the late 1980s, and the intergovernmental groups such as Schengen and Trevi and the Ad Hoc Group of EC immigration ministers worked to that end.[3] The 'porous' states making up Europe's southern rim (those for whom immigration control was not yet seen as vital to national survival) were funded, courted and told to tighten their immigration controls, physical and bureaucratic. **Spain**, for example, received EC funding to improve coastal security, to protect its more than 200 sea harbours from illegal incursions and to fortify its north African enclaves of Ceuta and Melilla with the latest electronic border control security measures. Under the guidance of the northern European states, amnesties for illegal immigrants were followed by strict immigration controls criminalising migration for work (except temporary and seasonal work).

These measures were to bring southern Europe roughly into line with the north in terms of treatment of immigration and asylum: the laissez-faire attitude of the south, tolerating illegals for the work they did, was to go. The south was, after all, the gateway to Europe 'proper'.

The work of the intergovernmental groups went further. They defined common criteria for the entry of foreign visitors into the territory of the EC and provided for the setting up of an information exchange system, by means of which each country would alert the others to the existence, and identifying particulars, of 'undesirables' who were not to be admitted: those who had breached immigration controls in the past, or who had committed crimes, or who were *suspected* of planning to commit crimes. They drew up lists of countries whose citizens would have to apply in advance for visas to enter the territory: not only were individuals suspect, but whole nationalities. The common list, transferred in 1993 to EU competence by the Maastricht treaty, now contains 129 countries, including most African and Asian nations.

The detailed provisions worked out by the intergovernmental groups to secure the fences of Europe are set out in the Schengen supplementary agreement of June 1990, which nine EU states have signed (all but the UK, Ireland and Denmark). The Schengen provisions have been carried wholesale into other intergovernmental agreements signed or to be signed by all twelve EU member states. The External Borders Convention (awaiting signature for two years but held up because of Anglo-Spanish disputes over Gibraltar) contains the provisions for visas, information exchange and external border controls. It also provides for all member states to introduce carrier sanctions, to penalise airlines and shipping companies for carrying undocumented passengers or passengers with false documents.[4]

Visa controls and carrier sanctions have been standard parts of northern Europe's armoury against refugees since 1986/7. Whenever a particular country began to produce a large exodus of refugees, visa controls were imposed. The **UK** imposed a visa requirement on people from Sri Lanka in 1985, those from Turkey in 1989, those from Uganda in 1991 – each time in response to a refugee crisis in the country of origin. The effect was to prevent refugees from arriving; they could not get refugee visas (in UK law there is no such thing), and so (because of carrier sanctions) could not board the flights or ships to get them out of their country.

Carrier sanctions forced transport companies into an immigration control function on pain of fines which, in the UK, went up from £1,000 to £2,000 per passenger in August 1992. Some £30m has been paid by airlines in the UK since the law was introduced in 1987. The fines have resulted in stringent controls at airline desks in all international airports. To board a plane in Moscow bound for western Europe, for example, each passenger must now go through three separate passport checks. At Lisbon airport, the national airline of **Portugal**, TAP, has since October 1991 photocopied the passports of all non-white passengers travelling to the UK, Germany, the US and Canada, since, a spokesman said, they were all 'potential clandestine immigrants'.

These measures also created a huge market for profiteers, who, in exchange for refugees' life savings, forge travel documents or simply smuggle their customers – overland or in leaky boats or as stowaways in cargo ships – to Europe. Many hundreds have drowned when tiny, overloaded fishing boats have gone down in the Straits of Gibraltar. In February 1994, a sealed container was opened in Felixstowe, England, to reveal the bodies of four Romanian stowaways who had died breathing the toxic fumes used to clean the container. A fifth man, who survived, was detained and ordered to be returned to France, which had rejected his asylum claim.[5] In the same month, another sealed container opened in Sweden was found to contain sixty-four stowaways from Iraq, including twenty-four children. Each had paid US$2,500. There was hardly any oxygen left in the container, and the air temperature inside was 70°C.[6] Stowaways are not welcomed if they are discovered by ships' captains; some have paid with their lives, being killed and their bodies thrown overboard by captains anxious to avoid fines, while others have been imprisoned on board ship and denied the chance to claim asylum in any European port. European immigration officers have been known to collude in this violation of the Geneva Convention.

Pass the Parcel

A grim game of 'pass the parcel' has grown up in respect of asylum-seekers arriving in western Europe. The Dublin agreement, signed by the twelve EC states in 1990 (and once again lifted wholesale from the Schengen Accord), introduced the idea that asylum-seekers coming to western Europe could only apply for asylum to one European country and that, once refused by one, they could be rejected by all. It defined the state responsible for processing an asylum claim as the one which the passenger had first arrived in, whether lawfully or not. The result of the agreement is that all asylum-seekers who arrive in the **UK** at Dover, for example, are returned to **Belgium** or **France** without their asylum claim being considered. Thus, a Ugandan woman, who arrived at Dover with her young child after flying into Paris and taking the train to London, was refused permission to claim asylum in Britain. Her parents and husband had been killed, the latter in front of her, and she had been raped by soldiers and tortured. She was undergoing a nervous breakdown. Her only surviving relative, her adult sister, was here. Only after threats of legal action did the Home Office change its mind and allow her to have her asylum claim processed.[7]

The above example could be multiplied by a factor of thousands and would still not do justice to the degradation, misery and hardship caused to asylum-seekers by the so-called 'RIO phenomenon' ('Refugees in Orbit').'Only a little day trip; hardly a major expedition – a matter of discomfort not danger', is the way the shuttling of asylum-seekers from airport to airport has been described by British judges. A Somali refugee who collapsed on arrival in the **UK** and was found to have shrapnel lodged in his head and neck was not treated for his injuries other than being given paracetamol, and was returned to **Italy**, because he had spent two hours in the transit lounge at Rome airport on his way to Britain.[8]

The creation of buffer zones

The disintegration of the Communist bloc in central and eastern Europe provided both a new potential source of 'economic migrants' to the west and a new overland route for them and other refugees to get there. The response of the western European states has been twofold: the hasty creation of a new iron curtain to keep out their eastern neighbours; and the signing of agreements whereby the 'hinterland' countries assume responsibility for all immigration policing of the eastern avenue to the EU.

Austria has, since 1990, deployed 2,000 military personnel on its borders. In the first half of 1993, they turned away 77,000 undocumented refugees.

Germany's constitution prevented the turning away of refugees at the borders. The murderous events of Hoyerswerda, Rostock, Mölln and Solingen formed the perverse rationale for German politicians' removal of the constitutional right to asylum, enabling Germany to turn away many asylum-seekers at the borders without considering their claims. Anyone arriving from a 'safe' country (the German authorities have compiled a list) can be sent back there.

Germany's lead in abolishing constitutional safeguards in the face of the 'menace' of refugees was followed by **France** where, in November 1993, a law amending the French constitution along similar lines was introduced. Since the introduction of the new asylum law in Germany in mid-1993, asylum applications there have dropped by more than half. Anyone coming from, or through, **Poland** is returned there instantly under a bilateral agreement which gives Poland the responsibility for the processing, detention and removal of asylum-seekers and immigrants of all nationalities who use Poland as a stepping-stone into Germany. In exchange, Poland receives financial assistance. In fact, the agreement represents the contracting-out of immigration and refugee control of Germany's eastern borders to Polish immigration police.

In 1992, **Spain** signed a similar agreement with **Morocco**, under which 2,000 Moroccan troops guarded the coastline of Morocco to ensure that the refugee-carrying boats could not leave. The Moroccan authorities imprisoned Africans who were suspected of wanting to cross into Europe. In October 1993, ten children aged between 10 and 17, who stowed away on a ship leaving Morocco bound for Spain, were summarily returned on arrival in Spain. At first, the Spanish authorities refused even to allow the children to leave the ship, and then they detained them and claimed that they were not asylum-seekers and that their parents had been in touch and wanted them back. The children were put back on the ship and sent to Tangier, where no one claimed them and they were detained by the Moroccan authorities. Spanish anti-racists formed a broad anti-deportation front in the wake of the children's removal, accusing their government of deception and of allowing political and diplomatic considerations to weigh over humanitarian ones. Spain's prime minister had earlier described the illegal entry of immigrants and refugees from north Africa as 'the key problem facing Spain and the EC'.

It was in the context of this fear, graphically expressed by other western European leaders, of millions of refugees 'flooding' into their territory via central and eastern Europe and via the Maghreb into Spain – that these 'peripheral' states were recruited as agents of western European immigration control. A parallel Dublin convention has now been drafted and awaits signature by some or all of the EFTA states – **Norway**, **Sweden**, **Finland**, **Austria**, **Switzerland**, **Iceland** and **Liechtenstein** (of which all but Switzerland are part of the European Economic Area) and states of central and eastern Europe. But while the Dublin convention at least envisaged that all member states would be signatories to the Geneva Convention on Refugees, no such assumption can be made about the states signing the parallel convention.

But the countries of western Europe are not waiting for that convention. By March 1994, a plethora of bilateral and multilateral readmission agreements had been signed between western and eastern European states providing for 'mutual' readmission of each other's immigrants.[9] In practice, of course, the flow is all one way. Thus, the Schengen states signed an agreement with **Poland** in 1991 obliging the latter country to take back refugees arriving in a Schengen country having transited through Poland. **Austria** has signed agreements with **Hungary**, **Poland**, **Romania**, **Slovenia** and the **Czech Republic**; **Belgium** has signed similar agreements with **Poland**, **Romania** and **Slovenia**. **Denmark** has agreements with **Latvia** and **Lithuania**. **France** has agreements with **Poland**, **Romania** and **Slovenia**. In addition to the German-Polish agreement of 1993, **Germany** has signed an agreement with **Romania**, which paved the way for the deportation of around 10,000 Romanies in 1992, after their asylum claims were rejected. In November 1993, the International Federation of Human Rights called on Germany to suspend the repatriation accord in the light of the lynchings, manhunts and burning of homes of Romanies in Romania.

Italy has signed an agreement with **Poland** and is negotiating with **Slovenia**, in addition to the financial and technical aid it provides to **Albania** under an agreement entered in 1991, after the summary and probably illegal removal of thousands of Albanians. The **Netherlands** and **Luxembourg** were negotiating agreements with **Poland** and **Slovenia** in June 1993. **Norway** has an agreement with **Lithuania**, **Spain** with **Poland**, and **Sweden** is negotiating with **Poland** and **Romania**, while cooperating informally with the **Baltic states**. **Switzerland** has an agreement with **Hungary**, mainly to secure the return of Kosovo Albanians, and is preparing a similar agreement with **Romania**.

Immigration control in the buffer states

The agreements by the peripheral states to act as buffer zones to prevent the entry of immigrants and refugees into the west have had a knock-on effect on their own immigration and asylum policies. At a meeting in Prague in March 1993, **Austria, Hungary, Poland**, the **Czech** and **Slovak Republics** and **Slovenia** agreed to sign accords on mutual readmission of 'illegal entrants'. The six countries agreed to harmonise immigration rules, to clamp down on smuggling of refugees, and to strengthen their border controls. Those coming to **Poland** from **Romania, Bulgaria** and most countries of the former **USSR** are now only admitted with an officially registered invitation from a Polish citizen, and the Polish authorities arrested over 18,000 people for attempted illegal entry in 1993. The **Czech Republic** has been denounced by Amnesty International for the toughness of its new asylum criteria and procedures introduced in December 1993. It has also formulated strict new rules for those travelling from **Romania, Bulgaria, Ukraine** and the former **USSR** and **Yugoslavia**, and has introduced new citizenship laws which render many Romanies in the country stateless and liable to expulsion to **Slovakia**. Slovakia refused entry to nearly 20,000 people in the first half of 1993, from China, Vietnam, other parts of Asia and Africa as well as Europe. **Hungary** refused entry to a million foreigners at its borders in 1992. Its border police use sniffer dogs to search for humans concealed in the freight carried by trucks.

Conditions in the detention camps established by some of the central and eastern European states are said to be grim. At the end of 1992, **Poland** was holding thousands of Romanies from Romania who were suspected of wanting to cross the Elbe into Germany. In **Hungary**, where refugees from outside Europe are not recognised, there are periodic swoops on African, Arab, Chinese and Romanian people who are suspected of being illegal immigrants. More than 1,000 were detained in one swoop in 1992, of whom 740 were expelled immediately on chartered flights to Damascus, Hanoi and elsewhere, while another 400 were held in detention camps. Later in the year, Amnesty International was refused access to the camp to check allegations that inmates had been beaten unconscious and that teargas was used to quell riots.

The United Nations High Commissioner for Refugees has expressed fears that the new level of cooperation between European countries, east and west, will result in many genuine victims of persecution being effectively shut out of Europe or being returned to countries of persecution.[10] Even among countries which have signed the Geneva convention, there is no common understanding on its interpretation, no European court of justice to adjudicate on unjustified refusals. Many asylum-seekers are simply being shipped back with no opportunity to seek protection. But the process of cooperation continues and intensifies. The Berlin group, named after its first meeting in Berlin in October 1991, brought together ministers of thirty-three European countries to look at ways of coordinating immigration control across the whole of Europe and, in particular, ways of combating clandestine immigration. It met again in Budapest in February 1993 and discussed enlarging the Schengen-Poland agreement to bring in more eastern European states such as **Hungary**, the **Czech** and **Slovak Republics** and **Romania**. In June 1993, the 'Vienna Group', 'senior officials entrusted with the follow-up to the Conference of ministers on the movement of persons coming from central and eastern European countries', met at Strasbourg under the auspices of the Council of Europe to discuss 'solidarity and burden-sharing' in relation to refugees coming from or through eastern Europe to the west. The solidarity, however, was not with the refugees. The working paper of the meeting[11] talks of 'the need for reinforced collective cooperation to prevent disorderly movements from occurring'. The 'disorderly movements' are the refugees. 'Pressure', the document remarks, 'will always be exerted on the weakest link of the chain': the solution is yet stronger immigration controls in all the states of the east. To that end, interested western governments have already given assistance, equipment and training to immigration officials in eastern and central Europe: a chart reveals that **Austria**, for example, has provided **Hungary** with patrol cars, while **Sweden** and **Finland** have sent patrol boats to the Baltic states and Sweden has provided training to Baltic officials, resulting in most ships being stopped and refugees apprehended before their arrival in Sweden. The **USA** has sent computer equipment to **Hungary** and given training to immigration officials in the **Czech Republic**, **Russia** and **Slovenia**. **Hungary** has put in a request to western donors for 200 automated travel document scanners and 300 UV-IR lamps, while the **Czech Republic** has requested security laminate verifiers and videospectral comparators.[12]

Associated states

Incentives for the states of central and eastern Europe to take on the burden of readmitting asylum-seekers under these agreements are not hard to find.[13] They all want membership of the EU and access to EU markets and investment. They get limited access to EU markets, as well as limited opportunities for work in the EU for some of their nationals, through Association Agreements. The EU has had such agreements for many years with the Maghreb countries, **Turkey** and **ex-Yugoslavia**; in 1992 Association Agreements were signed with **Poland**, **Hungary** and **Czechoslovakia**. **Bulgaria** and **Romania** have similar agreements. Their ambition to join the EU is not forgotten, either: at the Copenhagen summit of June 1993 ministers drew up an agreement with these six 'Visograd' countries (they are six with the separation of the Czech and Slovak republics) which expressed 'the commitment to work for the gradual enlargement of the community to eastern Europe in the years to come'. In March 1994, **Hungary** and **Poland** signalled their intention to make formal applications to join the EU.

The club of civilised nations

The buffer states have been encouraged by the EU to sign the Geneva Convention on Refugees and its Protocol, to apply for membership of the Council of Europe and to sign and ratify the European Convention on Human Rights. So far, **Bulgaria**, the **Czech Republic, Estonia, Hungary, Lithuania, Poland, Romania, Slovakia** and **Slovenia** have joined the Council of Europe, and **Albania, Belarus, Croatia, Latvia, Moldova, Russia** and **Ukraine** have applied to join and have been granted special guest status with the Council's parliamentary assembly. **Bulgaria**, the **Czech Republic, Hungary, Poland** and **Slovakia** have signed the European Convention on Human Rights.

These actions will, according to official thinking, render the countries safe and civilised, and therefore no one will be able to complain about being sent back there. It is the idea of the 'safe country' which is the key to current refugee policy in Europe. For while the Geneva Convention prohibits the return of refugees to countries where they fear persecution, it does not prevent their forced return to countries which are deemed safe – whether these are countries the refugees have fled from or countries through which they have passed.

The 'safe country' policy

The original plan of the western European governments, led by Britain, was to declare all countries which had signed basic human rights declarations such as the European Convention on Human Rights 'safe', and thus all refugees from such countries 'bogus' or 'manifestly unfounded' – and send them back there. The plan, exposed in a secret document from the Ad Hoc group which was leaked in June 1992, caused outrage. Critics pointed to Turkey as a local example of a signatory of the ECHR which practises torture on political dissidents. When it was finally agreed by European immigration ministers meeting in London in November 1992, the concept of a 'safe country' was not quite so crude, but the essentials were retained. The resolution adopted by the ministers[14] agreed that asylum-seekers from 'safe' countries, or who had travelled through a 'safe' country, should have their applications declared 'manifestly unfounded' and be subjected to an accelerated procedure which would ensure their removal from the country within a month.

The accompanying resolution on 'manifestly unfounded' asylum claims singled out for the accelerated procedure asylum-seekers who had not sought the protection of their own country's authorities or had failed to move to a safer part of their country, or who had failed to claim asylum in a neighbouring country. Those who had left their own continent to seek asylum were to be regarded with the most scepticism. 'Inter-continental movements are seldom necessary for protection', the document declared, condemning as 'unlawful' the actions of asylum-seekers who did not avail themselves of local protection but travelled to another continent.[15]

The documents together revealed the aims of the European immigration ministers as the eventual withdrawal of protection from refugees from outside Europe (reversing the process which extended recognition to non-European refugees in 1967), and the re-defining of more and more areas as 'safe' for refugees to return to. Although the ministers disclaimed any intention to draw up a common list of 'safe' countries at the November 1992 meeting, they created an 'information bank' and exchange system, CIREA (the centre for information, discussion and exchange on asylum), on which all member states are expected to draw in deciding which countries are 'safe'. Refugee groups and others such as Amnesty International and the UN High Commission for Refugees will have no access to the material held by CIREA, so no one will be able to assess the criteria or the information used to declare countries 'safe'. **Germany** has already begun drawing up its own list: thus, asylum-seekers who come from or through Ghana or Romania, for example, will be deemed 'manifestly unfounded' unless they have overwhelming proof to the contrary. The clear intention behind the European initiatives is to be able to declare most of the world 'safe' for asylum-seekers, whatever the reality.

According to the logic of expediency of western Europe, Romania is 'safe' for the Romanies, despite the lynchings and man-hunts; Kosovo is 'safe' for the ethnic Albanians, just as Sri Lanka is safe for Tamils and Sarajevo will soon be safe for the Bosnians. So, **Switzerland** has signed an agreement with **Sri Lanka** whereby rejected Tamil asylum-seekers will be repatriated against their will back to Sri Lanka. The **Netherlands** has signed a special agreement with **Vietnam** enabling 350 rejected asylum-seekers to be returned to Vietnam, in exchange for economic assistance to the country. **Belgium** has signed similar agreements with **Morocco** and **Ghana**. And **Austria**'s interior minister organised a secret meeting in March 1994 with his counterparts in **Germany**, **Switzerland**, **Denmark**, **Sweden**, **Norway** and **Macedonia** to plan the repatriation of ethnic Albanian asylum-seekers to Kosovo.[16]

The true intention of those framing European asylum policies was expressed in the recommendation of the Budapest meeting of February 1993. Dealing with those readmitted into an eastern European country with no right of residence there, the meeting recommended that they should be 'returned without delay to the country of origin or where they began their journey, and, in particular, to countries which are far away'.[17]

References

1 The Geneva Convention on the status of refugees, drawn up in 1951, and the Protocol of 1967 which removed the territorial limitation to refugees from European countries.

2 House of Lords: Select Committee on the European Communities, Report and Minutes of Evidence, 1988.

3 For further information about the work of these groups and their role in the creation of the new Europe, see 'Variations on a theme of racism', *Race & Class* Vol 32 no 3, 1991, and *Statewatching the new Europe*, Statewatch, 1993.

4 The External Borders Convention, drafted by the Ad Hoc Group on Immigration. The European Commission has just presented a proposal to break the log-jam over Gibraltar which would allow disputes under the Convention to be referred to the European Court of Justice. The proposal would make immigration control too accountable for some states, including Britain.

5 *Guardian* 4.2.94.

6 *Migration Newssheet* March 1994.

7 This and other accounts of court cases come from case files.

8 Case file; *CARF* No 14, May 1993.

9 Much of the information in this paragraph is from the Report of the Working Party on a Solidarity Structure (see note 11 below).

10 In its annual report presented in January 1994, UNHCR commented that 'the tradition of asylum seems to be collapsing' in Europe. The Geneva Convention was now 'insufficient' to protect refugees, it commented (the Convention excludes war and civil war refugees).

11 Report of the Working party on a Solidarity Structure (Burden-sharing) of the Group of senior officials entrusted with the follow-up to the Conference of Ministers on the movement of persons coming from central and eastern European countries (Vienna Group), Strasbourg, 3 June 1993, Council of Europe.
12 *Ibid.*
13 The linkage between the contracting out of immigration control and trade and aid benefits was made explicit in the European Commission's 2nd Communication on Immigration and Asylum, produced in February 1994. In addition, the Netherlands government announced in January 1994 that it is to include a provision on readmission of rejected asylum-seekers in all bilateral agreements signed with refugee-producing or transit countries.
14 Resolution concerning host third countries, and Conclusions on countries in which there is generally no serious risk of persecution, Ad Hoc Group on Immigration, London, 30 November 1992.
15 Resolution on manifestly unfounded applications for asylum, Ad Hoc Group on Immigration, London, 30 November 1992.
16 *Independent* 18.3.94.
17 Working paper on a solidarity structure (see note 11).

3 Country summaries

AUSTRIA (EFTA, EEA, and has applied to join EU and
Schengen Group)
Population: 7.8m (600,000 non-citizens)
Basis of citizenship: By descent. Naturalisation possible, strict
conditions.

Immigration and asylum
Asylum-seekers: 76,200 asylum-seekers 1992 (including 60,000
Bosnians), 75 per cent from central and eastern Europe.
Law and practice: Under the asylum law of June 1992, refugees with no
identification, or no proof of persecution, and those who had travelled
through a 'safe' country are summarily rejected by border police.
Amnesty International condemned the law, which has resulted in the
removal of protection of asylum-seekers against *refoulement* and
violates the Geneva Convention, in a report of November 1993.
In July 1993, a new Residency Act came into force, introducing strict
income and accommodation criteria for the issue and renewal of
residence permits to foreigners. It has resulted in thousands being
threatened with deportation for claiming benefits, living in too small a
room or failing to renew residence permits in time. Children born in
Austria but not entered in their parents' passport have also been
threatened with deportation.
In March 1994, Austria's Interior Ministry called a secret meeting with
representatives from the German, Swiss, Danish, Swedish, Norwegian
and Macedonian governments, to organise the forced repatriation of
Kosovo Albanian asylum-seekers.

Racism and fascism
Legislation: Constitutional law against the formation of nazi parties.
Electoral parties: FREIHEITLICHE PARTEI ÖSTERREICHS (FPÖ). Founded
1955. Led by Jörg Haider. Austria's third largest party, the Freedom
Party stands for pan-German nationalism, is anti-immigration and

denies Austria's nazi past. Until February 1993 it had thirty-three seats in parliament (16.6 per cent of vote), but five MPs left, claiming it was too extreme, to form rival party. In winter 1992, FPÖ launched its 'Austria First Petition', a twelve-point programme that called for, among other things, tightening of Austria's refugee laws, identity cards for foreigners, and quotas on the numbers of foreign children in classrooms. Four hundred and seventeen thousand people signed the petition which, although fewer than anticipated, was enough to trigger a parliamentary debate. In January 1993, the FPÖ won 20 per cent of the vote in municipal elections in Graz, Austria's second largest city. In three provincial elections in March 1994, the FPÖ increased its share of the vote in the states of Tyrol, Salzburg and Carinthia by an average of more than 2.5 per cent on 1989.

Other parties: Small neo-nazi parties include the NATIONALISTISCHE FRONT, said to be assembling the nucleus of a highly-centralised terror organisation called the NATIONALES EINSATZKOMMANDO (NEK), and the POPULAR EXTRA-PARLIAMENTARY OPPOSITION (VAPO), a paramilitary neo-nazi organisation whose leader, Gottfried Küssel, was jailed for ten years in September 1993 for seeking to re-establish a nazi state in Austria. In 1986, the Austrian constitutional court ruled against the formation of nazi parties, but in February 1992 the laws were relaxed so as to make penalties less severe.

Racial violence: Throughout 1992, refugee hostels were firebombed. After an attack on one centre in Gutenstein, near Vienna, in September, the mayors of Salzburg and Vienna did not condemn the violence but announced instead that they would take in no more refugees. At the end of 1993, the far Right launched a letter-bomb campaign against Left figures and people working with refugees.

BELGIUM (EU, Schengen)

Population: 9.9m (0.9m non-Belgian). 85,000 Turks, 142,000 Moroccans, 62,000 other Africans and Asians.

Basis of citizenship: By descent (no right of citizenship by birth in Belgium). Children born in Belgium to parents born in Belgium may apply to register. Naturalisation: criteria for full naturalisation very strict.

Immigration and asylum

Asylum-seekers: 26,800 asylum-seekers 1993.

Law and practice: Restrictive asylum laws impose tough criteria and exclude those without documents and others from asylum.

A new detention centre was opened at Zaventem airport (Brussels) in 1992 for asylum-seekers, and another was opened in December 1993. Four hundred and fifty extra places were to be made available in 'holding centres' for deportees.

The Belgian state was found guilty by administrative courts three times in 1993 of subjecting asylum-seekers to inhuman and degrading treatment and violating their legal rights.

Interior minister Tobback said after the latest case in December 1993, 'It won't be the last time.'

The 'Tobback' law of 1993 allowed for the summary rejection of asylum claims at the border, the speeding up of appeals, the detention of asylum-seekers and other foreigners deemed dangerous to national security, and an increase in the period of administrative detention for deportees from one to two months. Further provisions cut off social assistance to asylum-seekers automatically once their asylum claim is rejected, tightened conditions for family visits and allowed the computerised storage and comparison of asylum-seekers' fingerprints. A 'vigorous' policy of expulsion of rejected asylum-seekers resulted in a doubling of the percentage of expulsion orders carried out in 1993.

In February 1994, readmission agreements were concluded with Ghana, Romania and Morocco.

Racism and fascism

Legislation: Criminal law prohibits racial discrimination in public places, incitement to racial hatred or to discrimination; a January 1994 draft bill proposes to extend the law to employment and housing.

Electoral parties: VLAAMS BLOK (VB), Founded 1979. Led by Karel Dillen. Stands for Flemish nationalism, anti-immigration (popular slogan used is 'Our own people first') and an amnesty for second world war nazi collaborators. In 1991 elections, won twelve seats in the Chamber of Representatives and five seats in the senate (6.6 per cent of vote). Won 25 per cent of vote in Antwerp. Has one MEP on the European Parliament's Technical Group of the European Right. In 1992, published 'Immigration: the solutions', a seventy-point strategy based on Le Pen's programme of 'National Preference'.

FRONT NATIONAL (FN), Founded 1983. Led by Daniel Feret. The FN, which campaigns against immigration and for strong law and order policies, is a sister organisation to the French FN. Has one seat in the Chamber of Representatives.

Other parties: Many small, neo-nazi and skinhead groups involved in attacks on Left and immigrant targets. In a rare prosecution which ended in September 1993, eight members of L'ASSAUT (Attack) were sentenced to eighteen months' imprisonment for paramilitary activities after a series of brutal attacks on migrants in 1991 and 1992, and after a stockpile of illegal weapons was found. In September 1993, the VLAAMSE MILITANTE ORDRE (VMO), banned in the 1980s for its violence, was re-founded.

Racial violence: Seems to be linked to areas where far Right is influential. In Antwerp, in November 1992, three Moroccans were injured after an attack at a cafe. In 1993, there were racist killings in Liège and Brussels. In January 1994, a soldier convicted of an arson attack on an asylum hostel in August 1993 was sentenced to three years' imprisonment, two suspended, after the military court decided the attack was not racist.

Police: In 1992, four 'immigrant' youths died in situations arising out of contact with the police. In December 1992, public disquiet arose after three plain-clothes police officers were sentenced to just six months' imprisonment for a violent assault on a Pakistani man who did not produce his identity papers 'quickly' enough. But in 1993 Brussels police were given new public order powers, including rapid response units, horse and dog patrols.

CZECH REPUBLIC (Association Agreement with EU)
Population: 10.4m (about 200,000 Romanies).
Basis of citizenship: Was *ius soli* (right to citizenship by birth on territory). New laws remove Czech citizenship retrospectively from many Romanies long resident in the country.

Immigration and asylum
Asylum-seekers: 1,700 in 1993 (39 nationalities).
Law and practice: Part of Czechoslovakia until 1993. In 1990, the government announced the 'gradual repatriation' of 37,000 Vietnamese guestworkers admitted during Communist rule. An agreement signed with Vietnam in 1991 enabled 17,000 to be repatriated.

In the first quarter of 1993, over 12,000 people were arrested as illegal immigrants at the borders, 90 per cent of whom were in transit for Germany.

December 1993: asylum law amended so that authorities can reject claimants from 'safe' countries or those with 'apparently unjustifiable' claims. Law also demands that asylum is claimed immediately at the border and shortens appeal times. Amnesty International denounced the new law as 'violating international norms of protection', while UNHCR expressed concern.

January 1994: visa requirements imposed on passengers from former Yugoslav and Soviet Union republics.

Racism and fascism
Electoral parties: REPUBLICAN PARTY, led by Dr Miroslav Sladek. Inspired by German party of the same name, the RP calls for expulsion of Vietnamese and Cuban guestworkers, more law and order, and the resettlement of Gypsies. In June 1992 elections, gained 6 per cent of vote.
Other parties: Skinhead activity increasing, particularly around neo-nazi music scene.
Racist violence: At least twelve Romanies known to have died in racist violence in 1992 in Czechoslovakia. Vietnamese workers and African students also complain of constant harassment. September 1993: four Romanies killed in or escaping racist attacks.

DENMARK (EU, Nordic Union)
Population: 5.1m (0.1m non-Danish). 30,000 Turks, 7,000 Africans, 38,000 Asians.
Basis of citizenship: By descent. Naturalisation possible for those with seven years' residence, perfect Danish, no debts to state, and for those married to Danish citizens for two years.

Immigration and asylum
Asylum-seekers: 17,300 asylum-seekers 1993 (excluding 11,000 'war refugees' from former Yugoslavia given temporary protection).
Law and practice: Restrictive asylum laws allow fast-track processing of 'manifestly unfounded' applications, expulsion of those without visas to 'safe' third countries, fines on airlines bringing them, fingerprinting of those whose identity is doubtful. Anchored ships are used as reception/detention centres.
In 1992, there were proposals to remove family reunion rights from non-Danish citizens, to extend the probationary period before spouses of Danish citizens were given residence rights from two to four years, and to adopt more stringent criteria for naturalisation, which would exclude those who had committed minor criminal offences. In early 1993, the prime minister resigned as a result of disclosures that applications in 1988/89 from relatives of Tamil refugees were deliberately delayed, causing the deaths of some family members waiting for permission to go to Denmark (the 'Tamilgate' scandal). The new coalition government pledged a more positive asylum policy.
In February 1994, a mass hunger strike by Tamils all over Denmark

followed the first deportation of a Tamil to Sri Lanka in eighteen months. In the same month, an extra eighty-six police were drafted in to check the documents of all passengers arriving from Nordic countries by ferry, at Germany's request, to prevent the 25,000 Kosovo Albanians expecting their asylum claims to be rejected in Sweden from travelling through Denmark to Germany to claim asylum there. In March, the government announced a new bill to speed up asylum procedures 'to spare the anguish of waiting'. The proposals include the abolition of some appeal rights.

Racism and fascism
Legislation: No general code. Laws against discrimination exclude housing and employment. Law prohibits incitement to hatred on basis of race, religion, gender.

Electoral parties: FREMSKRIDT PARTEIT (Progress Party). Founded 1972. Led by Mogens Glistrup. Proposals include the expulsion of all Muslims and refugees. Since 1988, when the Progress Party had sixteen seats in parliament, its influence has declined rapidly and it is no longer represented in parliament.

In May 1993, the CENTRE PARTY was formed as a break-away from the Christian Democrats. Disappointed by the CD's stance on immigration, the Centre Party aims to fight what it sees as moves towards making Denmark a multi-ethnic society.

Other parties: Several small neo-nazi organisations, most notably PARTEIT DE NATIONALE (PDN), led by Albert Larsen, known to have been involved in attacks on refugee centres and Left targets. In 1992, Danish Socialist Henrik Christensen was killed in a nazi firebomb attack.

Racial violence: Bomb attacks on asylum centres in 1992/93. Killing of 7-year-old refugee child by psychiatric patient in 1993 led to anger at failure to protect refugees.

Institutional violence: The report of a judicial inquiry into allegations made by two prison nurses in 1988 that asylum-seekers had been strapped down in special cells, where bright lights were kept on continuously, is still pending.

FINLAND (EFTA, Nordic Union, EEA, formal applicant to join EU)
Population: 5m
Basis of citizenship: By descent. Naturalisation possible on the basis of five years' residence and respectable character. Nordic citizens may naturalise after two years.

Immigration and asylum
Asylum-seekers: 3,500 asylum-seekers 1992 (half from former Yugoslavia, 1,500 Somali).
Law and practice: From 1990 the army was reinforced along the border with the Soviet Union and stringent passport checks were introduced to prevent immigration from there.
In July 1993, following the arrival of 108 Kurdish asylum-seekers by fishing boat via Estonia, the Aliens Act was amended to allow border police to reject refugees from countries deemed safe. The interior minister proposed in November 1993 to designate Estonia and Russia as safe countries, so as to allow the summary removal of asylum-seekers from these countries.

Racism and fascism
Racial violence: In 1993, the small village of Joensuu saw escalation of attacks on Somali refugees and Bangladeshi students. After a fight between Somalis and Finns, the police, who had previously ignored reports of racist violence, arrested just one Somali who allegedly used a knife during the fight and was subsequently jailed for one year.

FRANCE (EU, Schengen)
Population: 56.5m (3.5 non-French). 198,000 Turks, 500,000 Moroccans, 614,000 Algerians, 206,000 Tunisians, 200,000 other Africans, 227,000 Asians.
Basis of citizenship: Until 1993, by birth in France. New law 1993 requires those born in France of foreign parents to apply for citizenship and makes the granting of it discretionary. Naturalisation by residence and marriage also possible.

Immigration and asylum
Asylum-seekers: 26,500 asylum-seekers 1993 (10,900 from Africa, 7,400 from Europe). 27 per cent of applications granted.
Law and practice: Almost all non-EU citizens need visas to enter and conditions for visas have become increasingly stringent. Strict asylum laws include fast-track procedures for 'manifestly unfounded' claims, with no appeal rights before removal. In 1992, the practice of detaining asylum-seekers for up to twenty days at airports was legalised and a further law fined airlines and shipping companies which brought undocumented passengers. Seven African stowaways died after being thrown off a ship before it docked in France – so that the captain could avoid paying the fines.

1993: New government brought in policy of 'zero immigration': immigration laws amended to make detention and deportation easier, to allow police to check ID of anyone 'suspected of being foreign', to allow mayors to block 'suspect' marriages between French and foreign citizens, to make family reunion subject to stricter conditions. Laws condemned by Constitutional court, modified and re-presented.

November 1993: constitution amended to allow return of asylum-seekers to 'safe' countries without consideration of applications.

February 1994: A new police department is set up for the control of immigrants. DICILEC will deal with the entry, detection and expulsion of illegal immigrants. A new detention centre is to be built in Paris for 200 deportees. A readmission agreement is signed with Romania. Twenty thousand march through Paris protesting at the anti-immigrant measures.

Racism and fascism

Legislation: Code against discrimination in housing, employment, provision of services. Criminal laws against incitement to racial hatred, defamation and denial of holocaust. November 1993: a new law is introduced to punish racist abuse and hooliganism at football matches.

Electoral parties: FRONT NATIONAL. Founded 1972. Led by Jean Marie Le Pen. Anti-Arab and anti-Semitic, the FN calls for an end to the 'Islamification of France' and the repatriation of 'immigrants', and claims that the gas chambers were a mere detail of the second world war. In November 1991, FN launched its campaign of 'National Preference', outlining '50 measures against immigration' (said to resemble the 1933 Nuremberg laws).

Although the FN gained 12.5 per cent of the vote in the March 1993 general election, the electoral system is such that it has no seats in parliament (in fact it lost its one seat in Dreux, Normandy). Since the 1992 local elections, the FN has had 239 regional and 804 municipal councillors across France. Has ten MEPs.

Police: In 1992, the Federation Internationale des Droits des Hommes accused police of 'most shocking behaviour' towards immigrants, mostly in their abuse of identity-check powers. In January 1993, Council of Europe Commission on the Prevention of Torture urged French government to tighten procedures to protect suspects after hearing numerous allegations of police brutality. In November 1993, the Ligue des Droits des Hommes also condemned police's racist use of the new immigration powers.

Two north African youths died in 1992 after confrontations with police. Three north African youths were killed in April 1993, and a north African young woman was killed by police in October 1993. In addition, an Angolan man killed himself after being stopped for an identity check.

Institutional violence: In February 1993, the National Association for the Assistance of Foreigners at Frontiers criticised the violent methods whereby people were deported.

GERMANY (EU, Schengen)

Population: 79.7m (5.7m non-German). 1.7m Turkish, 198,000 African, 500,000 Asian.

Basis of citizenship: By descent through parents of German blood. By naturalisation: extremely limited and stringent. Bundestag currently debating easing of naturalisation conditions, particularly for second-generation 'immigrants' and for refugees.

Immigration and asylum

Asylum-seekers: 224,000 asylum-seekers Jan-June 1993; 98,000 July-Dec (new asylum law 1.7.93). Largest groups from Romania, former Yugoslavia, Bulgaria, Turkey. 500,000 applications processed 1993, of which 3.2 per cent granted.

Law and practice: Very strict immigration laws and deterrents for asylum-seekers from 1980s on.

1991: 'collection camps' set up for asylum-seekers with 'manifestly unfounded' claims, accelerated procedures introduced to cut down processing time to six weeks.

1992: fingerprinting of all asylum-seekers introduced; military personnel brought in to process claims. Thousands of Romanian gypsies deported under repatriation agreement with Romania.

1993: constitutional right to asylum modified to allow refusal of all coming through or from Europe, while those coming from any other country deemed 'safe' must provide compelling evidence of persecution. Appeal does not prevent removal from country. List of safe countries includes Romania, Bulgaria, Ghana, Pakistan. Agreement with Poland gives Poland responsibility for asylum-seekers arriving at German border.

Use of military radar and night vision devices to monitor eastern borders. Paramilitaries, including neo-nazis, patrol borders and help guards at Czech and Polish borders. Eight hundred people arrested each month on Polish border, and 1,600 per month on Czech border. November 1993: Plan to deport guestworkers invited to former East

Germany back to Angola, Mozambique and Vietnam discussed by regional governments. January 1994: Vietnamese died of burns having set fire to himself after asylum claim rejected.

March 1994: Plan to deport thousands of ethnic Albanians and others to former Yugoslavia is greeted with protests.

Racism and fascism

Legislation: Criminal laws against incitement to racial hatred. Anti-discrimination provisions in public service.

Only west European country refusing to ratify UN Resolution 62 on Protection of the Romany People. Federal Justice Ministry likely to bring in new laws to prosecute revisionism after Federal Court of Justice quashed race hatred conviction for Holocaust-denial in March 1994.

Electoral parties: REPUBLIKANER (REP). Founded 1983. Led by Franz Schönhuber. Stands for pan-German nationalism, is anti-immigration and claims to have growing support in armed forces. Schönhuber himself denounces 'immigrants' collectively as 'criminals'. Following April 1992 elections, REP has fifteen seats in regional parliaments (11 per cent of vote). It now has one member of the Bundestag, following Rudolf Krause's defection from the CDU. In March 1993 local elections in Hesse, it won 8 per cent of the vote. Its best result was in Frankfurt where it won ten seats on the city council (9.3 per cent of vote). It had six MEPs but splits have reduced the number to one; four are now non-aligned and one went to the DEUTSCHE LIGA, which is also represented in the Cologne council.

DEUTSCHE VOLKSUNION (DVU). Founded 1987. Led by Dr Gerhard Frey. Neo-fascist, the DVU is linked to the British revisionist historian, David Irving. Gained only 0.2 per cent of the vote in March 1993 local elections but is reported to have 23,000 members and has twelve seats in regional parliaments. In the September 1993 local elections, it got 3.2 per cent in Hamburg.

Both the Republikaner and the Deutsche Volksunion are attempting to expand their field of political influence into eastern Europe and the former Soviet bloc.

Other parties: Seventy-seven right-wing extremist organisations are being kept under observation, says Federal Office of Criminal Investigation. These groups have a total membership of 41,400. Four organisations, the German Comradeship League, the Nationalistische Front, National Offensive and the Deutsche Alternative, banned in 1993.

Racial violence: Attacks by 200 neo-nazis on refugee hostels in Rostock in August 1992 signalled start of a nationwide pogrom against refugees. Violence not confined to the east, as confirmed by statistics released by the Federal Criminal Police Office.

At least fifty-two people died in 1993 as a result of racist or fascist activities (arson attacks, stabbings, shootings, etc), of whom forty-one are believed to have been killed by members of the far Right. The victims included Turks, refugees, left-wing activists, the homeless, disabled, and people mistaken for Romanies. This compares with a documented twenty-two deaths in 1992.

Police/army: Police unwillingness to afford refugees protection against racist attacks has been confirmed by parliamentary investigative committee into the events of Rostock. Police have also been accused of violent behaviour. For instance, Amnesty International investigated allegations of police brutality at Granitz refugee camp after raid by riot police, as well as at refugee hostel in Bremen. Other asylum-seekers in Bremen alleged they were kicked, beaten and given electric shocks at the police station. Two refugees died in police custody in 1993. Further allegations of racism and criminality in Berlin's auxiliary police force as well as in police stations in Berlin.

German parliament's military ombudsman revealed in February 1993 that prosecutors were investigating forty-eight incidents involving right-wing soldiers.

GREECE (EU, Schengen)
Population: 10m (1m non-Greek). 19,000 African, 36,000 Asian.
Basis of citizenship: Birth on Greek soil to Greek parent, or ten years' residence.

Immigration and asylum
Asylum-seekers: 1,990 asylum-seekers allowed to register 1992 (77 per cent Iraqi), excluding 350,000 Albanians refused/expelled.

Law and practice: Since 1991 'exceptional measures' have been in place for policing of borders; 'crackdowns' on illegal immigrants have resulted in expulsion of hundreds of thousands of foreigners, mainly Albanians. In 1992, Greece joined Schengen group; passed new Aliens, Immigrants and Refugees law (the first since 1929), which set up 'anti-clandestine immigrant patrols', lists of 'undesirable aliens' and strict criteria for the issue of visas.

Several Iraqi refugees drowned attempting to reach Greece in small boats.

In 1993, police carried out a series of round-ups of 'illegal immigrants';

after a Greek priest was deported from Albania, 20,000 Albanians were detained and deported. In December 1993, the government was reported to be drafting new anti-illegal immigration measures.

Racism and fascism
Legislation: No general code. Penal law against discrimination (excludes housing, employment) and incitement.
Electoral parties: GREEK NATIONAL POLITICAL SOCIETY (EPEN). Founded 1984 as a vehicle for the ultra-right, authoritarian, imprisoned ex-dictator Giorgios Papadopoulous. It has little influence and has now lost its only seat in the national and European parliaments. Generally, Greek nationalism is on the increase, focusing particularly on the situation in Macedonia and the former Yugoslavia.
Other parties: HRYSSI AVGHI (HA): small but internationally active neo-nazi group. A group called GOLDEN DAWN was responsible for carving a swastika on a girl's face in November 1993.
Police: In February 1993 Greece's public order minister justified major police round-up of illegal immigrants whom he blamed collectively for crime. Crime statistics broken down to show crime rate amongst 'foreigners' greater than rest of population. Amnesty International alleged that Athens anti-narcotics police tortured refugees. Suleyman Akyar, a Turkish refugee, died in hospital eight days after his arrest in January 1991. Sehmus Ukus, a Turkish Kurd arrested in 1990, was allegedly beaten during interrogation and his feet and genitals burned with a cigarette lighter.

HUNGARY (Association Agreement with EU)
Population: 10.5m (1991)
Basis of citizenship: By descent; naturalisation on basis of marriage, permanent residence.

Immigration and asylum
Asylum-seekers: Recognises Europeans only as refugees and treats all non-Europeans as illegal entrants.
Law and practice: Has strengthened border controls and entry laws to prevent entry of 'illegal immigrants' in transit for Germany and Austria, and set up detention centres. In 1992, one million people were refused entry at the borders and 10,000 were detained in camps where conditions said to be 'appalling'. Round-ups of African, Arab, Chinese and Romanian people living in Hungary.

Racism and fascism

Legislation: Law of 1993 bans wearing of extremist symbols of Left or Right.

Electoral parties: Istvan Csurka, renowned for anti-Semitic statements, finally expelled from Magyar Democratic Forum in June 1993, along with three other right-wing MPs. Csurka now leads new party, the HUNGARIAN TRUTH AND LIFE PARTY, which has called for the creation of a 'Hungarian Christian nation-state with folk roots'.

Other parties: Growing concern about skinhead violence following violence in October 1992 when skinheads, dressed in Arrow Cross uniform (the post-war indigenous nazi party), disrupted a ceremony commemorating the Hungarian uprising of 1956. In November 1992, group of skinheads convicted of twenty-one acts of violence against Gypsies and foreigners, and in December 1992 members of the HUNGARIAN NATIONAL SOCIALIST ACTION GROUP, led by Istvan Gyorkos, convicted of incitement and possession of weapons following police raid.

Racial violence: Three Romanies killed in 1992 but government denied racial motivation. In September 1992, arson attacks on Romany homes in Ketegyhaza, on the Hungarian plain, described as the first pogrom against Hungarian Gypsies since the second world war. In November 1992, Martin Luther King Association documented 120 incidents, mainly against Arabs and Africans, since the beginning of 1992. Fifty-three Sudanese university students left the country in November 1992, saying they feared phsyical attack. In July 1993, Romanies marched in protest at neo-nazi violence against them in Egar.

Institutional violence: Amnesty International expressed concern about the situation at Kerepestarcsa detention camp near Budapest, following allegations of beatings and the use of teargas in confined spaces.

IRELAND (EU)

Population: 3.5m (0.1m non-Irish). No Africans or Asians.

Basis of citizenship: By birth in Ireland, and by descent.

Immigration and asylum

Asylum-seekers: Thirty-five applications for asylum 1991, of which three granted. Two hundred from former Yugoslavia accepted 1991/2.

Law and practice: Immigration dictated by very strict 1935 Aliens Act, giving unlimited powers of detention and deportation. Visa requirements imposed in line with UK. No formal refugee policy, but one in four asylum-seekers detained in prison.

Racism and fascism

Legislation: Incitement to racial hatred prohibited. Laws against unfair dismissal, but no provision for housing.

ITALY (EU, Schengen)

Population: 57.7m (0.7m non-Italian). 238,000 Africans, 140,000 Asians.

Basis of citizenship: Mixture of birth in country and descent: those born in Italy to Italian parents and those born to foreign parents and legally resident to age of majority can declare wish to become Italian.

Immigration and asylum

Asylum-seekers: 2,650 admitted to asylum procedures 1992.

Law and practice: Amnesties for irregular immigrants have been followed by tough immigration laws providing for deportation of irregular immigrants and those with no means of support, visa requirements, computerised registration of immigrants, quota system to tie immigration to labour market needs.

1992: decree that, other than family members and refugees, only temporary workers would be admitted, to 'retain the benefit of northern and sub-Saharan African labour without allowing for settlement'. Minister of justice proposed lower wage levels for non-EC migrant labour. 1994 quota of 60,000 foreigners announced, with strict controls to be kept on numbers.

1993: hundreds of illegal expulsions under decree providing immediate expulsion for foreigners accused of committing crimes, later declared unconstitutional, but re-presented in amended form.

New law January 1994 provides that foreigners dealing in contraband cigarettes are liable to be expelled.

Many complaints that Somali, Ethiopian and Eritrean war refugees were being returned without being allowed to claim asylum.

Racism and fascism

Legislation: New law 1993 against incitement to racial hatred.

Anti-discrimination laws cover employment, housing, health, treatment of detainees, implementing UN Convention against Racial Discrimination.

Electoral parties: NATIONAL ALLIANCE, formerly MOVIMENTO SOCIALE ITALIANO (MSI). Founded 1946. Led by Gianfranco Fini. Descended from Mussolini, the NA now declares itself 'post-fascist' (while Fini still praises Mussolini as greatest statesman of the century). Is nationalist, anti-communist and against immigration. In December 1993, came close to winning mayoral elections in Rome and Naples. Has four MEPs.

NORTHERN LEAGUE. Founded 1982 (then Lombard League). Led by Umberto Bossi. Anti-foreigner, corporatist, the NL moved from a position of secession to unity under a federal structure. In June 1993 mayoral council elections, it gained control of all the northern cities of Italy (except Turin). Has two MEPs.

In February 1994, the NA and the NL joined forces with the media magnate and multi-millionaire, Silvio Berlusconi, in FORZA ITALIA, which won 366 of the 630 parliamentary seats (42.9 per cent of the vote) in the March 1994 general election. The National Alliance, which gained some five million votes, more than doubled its share of the vote, from 5.4 per cent to 13.5 per cent. The Northern League's vote fell from 8.7 per cent to 8.4 per cent.

Other parties: Small neo-nazi parties include the Rome-based WESTERN POLITICAL MOVEMENT, known to have been involved in anti-Semitic actions. In 1993, the police carried out a series of raids directed against neo-nazi skinhead groups: the MOVIMENTO POLITICO in Rome, the AZIONE SKINHEAD in Milan and the FRONTE SKINHEAD in the Veneto region of north-east Italy were the main targets.

Racial violence: The influence of the far Right could be seen in the two murders in 1992, one of a homeless man. Many organised neo-nazi actions against irregular workers and Romanies, as well as desecration of Jewish cemeteries. The MSI put out anti-black posters and helped organise a shopkeepers' strike against the presence of immigrants in Caserta which led to several arson attacks against black people's property in June 1993.

July 1993: concerted attack on Africans and Asians in Genoa over several days.

September 1993: 500 African migrant workers forced to flee after locals in Puglia, south-eastern Italy, launch 'black hunt'. Estimated 100 racial attacks in Rome in first nine months of 1993.

Police: Carry out regular round-ups and raids on immigrants for deportation. Two immigrants shot dead by police in 1992. In February 1993, an Algerian immigrant was killed by police in Genoa at a road block. In September 1993, an 11-year-old Romany child was shot dead by police 'while attempting to escape'.

Institutional violence: Amnesty International recorded allegations of torture at Sollicciano prison, near Florence, where half prisoners are non-EU immigrants. In February 1993, security guards at a reception centre for immigrants were accused of torturing young immigrant, including burning his hands.

LUXEMBOURG (EU, Schengen)
Population: 0.38m (0.1m non-citizens). 1,700 Africans, 1,600 Asians.
Basis of citizenship: Birth in country to a parent born there.

Immigration and asylum
Asylum-seekers: 160 asylum-seekers 1991.
Law and practice: Strict immigration controls. Asylum-seekers coming through territory of other 'safe' countries returned. Family reunion for foreigners settled in country conditional on income and housing conditions.

NETHERLANDS (EU, Schengen)
Population: 15m (0.7m non-Dutch). 203,000 Turkish, 157,000 Moroccan.
Basis of citizenship: By birth in Netherlands to a Netherlands-born parent, or by naturalisation: requirements are five years' residence, no criminal record, integration into society (demonstrated by ability to speak language). Those married to Dutch citizens can apply after three years.

Immigration and asylum
Asylum-seekers: 35,400 in 1993, mainly from Yugoslavia, Iraq, Iran. 7,000 rejected asylum-seekers expelled.
Law and practice: Restrictive immigration policies (family reunion only); visas required from most countries. Military police handle asylum applications at ports and force is sometimes used to expel those summarily rejected. Fingerprinting and photographing of asylum-seekers.
1992: Twelve new 'investigation and reception centres' set up, with high fences, barred windows, electronic surveillance, where asylum-seekers obliged to stay. Accelerated procedures for 'manifestly unfounded' claims. Justice minister proposed to make family reunion rights of non-EC nationals conditional on income 'to curb inflow of West Indian youths'. Agreement with Dutch Caribbean islands to deport youths convicted of crime. Detention of foreigners in police stations pending expulsion approved.
Computerised aliens' administrative system set up, with identity,

residence and status of all foreigners. Linked to local registers. Police, tax authorities and social services have access.

1993: Cabinet approves measures denying welfare services, education or health care to those staying illegally.

January 1994: new immigration and asylum law in force. Imposes carrier sanctions. Asylum-seekers from countries designated 'safe' to be refused unless they have special reasons. Appeal rights restricted. Agreement signed with Vietnam to repatriate 350 rejected asylum-seekers, who fled from Czechoslovakia when that country decided to repatriate them. Bill introduced to deport families of immigrants who lose their jobs. Foreigners to require police permission to marry Dutch nationals. Carrying of ID cards to be compulsory from June 1994 for all over 12 years old.

Racism and fascism

Legislation: General code against racism, race discrimination and incitement. Includes measures against institutional racism and racism in employment and housing.

Electoral parties: CENTRUM DEMOCRATEN (1986), led by Hans Janmaat. Extreme right, racist and anti-immigration, it is developing links with the Belgian Vlaams Blok. Polls suggest that, if elections were held now, it would gain 3 per cent of national vote. In 1990 local elections, CD won fifteen council seats, principally in Rotterdam, Amsterdam and the Hague. In September 1992, some members split from CD to form NEDERLANDS BLOK. In March 1994 local elections, CD and CP'86 (see below) took eighty-six council seats, gaining over 10 per cent of the vote in Rotterdam, Utrecht and the Hague.

Other parties: CENTRUMPARTIJ '86: has links with German nazi NPD. Other small neo-nazi groups exist with a bonehead neo-nazi music scene emerging in 1992 around the fanzine *Hou Kontakt* ('Keep in touch').

Racial violence: One racist murder in 1992, although courts officially denied racial motivation. In January 1992, there was a wave of bomb attacks against migrant organisations and mosques, and physical attacks on foreigners. One racist murder in 1993. Additionally, a child was left to drown in a public park through onlookers' indifference; another child's murder was widely believed to result from racist failure to afford protection. One man was driven to suicide by racist harassment. In February 1994, five people were sentenced to between one and two years for their role in a series of forty-two racist attacks, including arson, in Nijmegen.

Police: In January 1993, a Turkish man died after being stopped by police. Concern about police harassment of immigrant youths during constant identity checks.

Institutional violence: Concern at methods deployed to deport refugees and treatment of refugees in centres after a woman refugee from Zaire, seven months pregnant, died in April 1992. In November 1992, riot police were deployed at Grenshospitium, a closed centre at Schiphol airport. Refugees claimed to be badly beaten and investigation was initiated. In August 1993, the minister of justice said that a Romanian asylum-seeker who had his mouth taped during an attempted deportation in 1992 and sustained brain damage would 'probably' receive compensation.

NORWAY (EFTA, EEA, Nordic Union. Has applied to join EU.)
Population: 4.26m. 130,000 foreign workers.
Basis of citizenship: By descent. Naturalisation possible after five to seven years. Spouses of Norwegian citizens may apply after two to four years.

Immigration and asylum
Asylum-seekers: 4,300 in 1992 (half from former Yugoslavia).
Law and practice: Strict immigration laws. Red Cross reception centres for refugees taken over by Directorate of Immigration in 1989. Very restrictive refugee policies. Centralised registration of asylum-seekers, with photographs and fingerprints. 1993: government announced decision to withdraw temporary protection from refugees from former Yugoslavia and started to deport 1,200 ethnic Albanians, and to implement stricter selection procedure for refugees. This led to many hunger-strikes and Albanians seeking sanctuary in Norwegian churches.

Racism and fascism
Electoral parties: FREMSKRITTSPARTIET (Progress Party) (1973). Led by Carl Hagen. Stands for stronger immigration controls. Progress Party official recently argued that only Christian immigrants should be allowed into Norway, urging the 'return' of all refugees to their home countries. Lost half its twenty-two parliamentary seats in the September 1993 general election.

Other parties: Norway has a myriad of small neo-nazi, revisionist organisations such as the PEOPLE'S MOVEMENT AGAINST IMMIGRATION and NORWEGIANS AGAINST IMMIGRATION, led by Arne Myrdal until he was imprisoned in 1993 for a violent assault on anti-racists. The FATHERLAND PARTY and END IMMIGRATION, two of these obscure parties, won 12,000 votes between them in the 1993 general election.

Racist violence: In 1992, terror attacks included a neo-nazi bombing of an immigrant school near Oslo, carried out by skinhead groups. A group called the BOOT BOYS is linked to WHITE ARYAN RESISTANCE and is believed to be behind many of the attacks.

POLAND (Association Agreement with EU)
Population: 37.8m (1991)
Basis of citizenship: By descent; naturalisation possible after five years' residence and in other defined circumstances.

Immigration and asylum
Law and practice: March 1991: signed agreement with Schengen states which obliged it to take back those illegally crossing from Poland into Schengen territory. New law allowed detention of foreigners caught trying to cross into Germany for up to ninety days (previously two days) and their expulsion from Poland; 13,500, mainly Romanians, caught attempting crossing, detained and returned.
1992: 33,500 arrested, vast majority Romanian. By end of 1992, estimated 100,000 Romanians waiting in Poland for opportunity to cross to the west. In 1993, 18,200 people arrested for attempted illegal entry. Agreement with Germany to take back all foreigners entering Germany through Poland (limited to 10,000 in 1993) in exchange for financial aid.

Racism and fascism
Electoral parties: No electoral party, although anti-Semitism is widespread in public life. Numerous neo-nazi organisations such as the openly anti-Semitic NATIONAL PARTY and a split from the NP, the NATIONAL PARTY SZCZERBIEC that only accepts as members Poles of the Christian faith. POLISH NATIONAL COMMUNITY – POLICE NATIONAL PARTY (Boleslaw Tejkowski) claims 4,000 members and uses skinheads as hit squads. German nazis from the NATIONALE OFFENSIVE accused of trying to agitate among the 350,000 ethnic Germans against the Polish state and for an *Anschluss* between Germany and Upper Silesia.
Fascist violence: In October 1992, Polish nazis beat to death a German lorry driver near Cracow. Desecration of Jewish cemeteries is linked to the level of openly anti-Semitic sentiment expressed both by politicians and the church.

PORTUGAL (EU, Schengen)

Population: 9.8m (0.1m non-Portuguese). 45,000 Africans, 4,000 Asians, 11,000 Brazilians.

Basis of citizenship: By descent, marriage to Portuguese citizen, naturalisation.

Immigration and asylum

Asylum-seekers: 600 registered 1992 (excludes those deemed 'manifestly unfounded', not permitted to register).

Law and practice: Screening procedure in place since 1983.

Signing of Schengen convention in 1991 followed by amnesty for irregular workers October 1992-January 1993 (under which 38,300 foreigners obtained residence permits). Simultaneously, Aliens Law 1992 provided for setting up of detention centres for illegal immigrants, imposition of visa requirements and refusal of permanent settlement except for refugees.

Border police (SEF) accused of turning back half of Angolans who arrived with visas, on grounds that they were suspected of being from Zaire, and of using violence to expel alleged illegal immigrants.

SEF admitted that Africans were targeted for most stringent checks at airports because of their 'incentive to migrate', but denied racism: 'We are not responsible for the fact that African passengers are black.' TAP admitted that since 1991, officials have photocopied passports of all non-white transit passengers, since they were all 'potential clandestine immigrants'.

1993: In January, eleven Brazilians detained in airport for three days with no beds or bathing facilities, then returned to Brazil. In June, Cabinet approved law to speed processing of asylum applications. September: bill provides for rejection and expulsion of all Romanian asylum-seekers.

Racism and fascism

Legislation: No anti-discrimination code, though constitution contains provisions for equality of treatment among Portuguese citizens.

Electoral parties: No parliamentary party of the extreme Right, but among the smaller neo-nazi organisations, CIRCULO EUROPEO DE AMIGOS DE EUROPEA (CEDADE), European Circle of Friends of Europe, is probably the most important.

Racial violence: Although not noted for experiencing the same levels of racial violence as the rest of Europe, racial harassment does exist. In June 1992, Africans complained of being too frightened to go out at night because of skinhead attacks. In 1990, skinhead violence had led to a government committee to monitor and study the situation of minorities in Portugal. Concern over fascist influence at football emerged following violence at a Benfica match in January 1993.

Police: One police killing of an immigrant in 1992 and many complaints of police authoritarianism and violence towards immigrants. In February 1993, the Brazilian government complained about the behaviour of frontier police at Lisbon's Potela airport. The detention of an Angolan woman and her child at Lisbon airport in February 1994 led to a four-day hunger strike by a priest, a ruling by a criminal court that the detention was unlawful and an appeal signed by 2,000 priests and brothers expressing their solidarity. Previously, in December 1991, Amnesty International had taken up the case of a white Angolan Portuguese citizen, who alleged he was violently beaten in a police station and called a 'worthless piece of Angolan shit'.

ROMANIA (Association Agreement with EU)
Population: 23.4m

Basis of citizenship: By descent. Naturalisation possible after five years' residence, conditional on adequate means, knowledge of language.

Racism and fascism

Widespread anti-Semitism in public life. The leader of the extreme-right GREATER ROMANIA PARTY, Corneliu Vadim Tudor, wrote an open letter to the president in April 1993 criticising him for attending the opening ceremony of the Holocaust museum in Washington, which he described as 'Satan's home'. The GREATER ROMANIA PARTY and the PARTY OF ROMANIAN NATIONAL UNITY have now been brought into Romania's coalition government.

The High Court has forbidden the distribution of the first Romanian translation of *Mein Kampf*.

Racial violence: The Society for Threatened People documented twenty known cases of pogroms against Romanian Gypsies in 1990 and 1991. In November 1993, the International Federation on Human Rights reported lynchings, manhunts and burning of homes of Romanies, and called on Germany to suspend the repatriation agreement allowing it to deport Romanies back to Romania.

SLOVAKIA (Association Agreement with EU)

Population: 5.3m (1 per cent Czech, 10.7 per cent Hungarian)
Basis of citizenship: *Ius soli* (birth on territory)

Immigration and asylum
See Czech Republic. Since Germany's asylum law changes, Slovakia
had 2,000 asylum-seekers detained in holding centres in July 1993 to
prevent them going on to Germany.

Racism and fascism
In September 1993, Slovak premier Vladimir Meciar described
Romanies as 'anti-social, mentally backward and socially un-
adaptable'. Now, ultra-nationalist SLOVAK NATIONAL PARTY has been
brought into new coalition government.

SPAIN (EU, Schengen)

Population: 39m (0.5m non-Spanish). 28,000 Moroccans, 10,000
other Africans, 75,000 central and south Americans, 36,000 Asians.
Basis of citizenship: Birth in Spain to a Spanish-born parent.

Immigration and asylum
Asylum-seekers: 12,600 in 1992.
Law and practice: Spain has become a 'gendarme of Europe' to keep
out immigrants and refugees from Africa. It has put in place
'implacable and systematic' policy of expulsion of rejected asylum-
seekers; set up marine guard to patrol coastline; fortified frontiers of
north African enclaves with barbed wire, closed-circuit TV, electronic
monitoring equipment; entered bilateral agreements with France to
control illegal entry of Turks and Africans.
1991: immigration amnesty followed by crackdown on illegal immigration, particularly from north Africa, described as 'the key problem
facing Spain and the EC'. Detention centres set up for those without
papers or lacking means of subsistence.
1992: thousands of people crossing straits of Gibraltar in small boats
arrested and expelled. Dozens drowned trying to make passage. Five
new ships with electronic detection facilities patrolled Spanish coast;
under agreement with Morocco, 2,500 men patrolled its coast to prevent departure of boats; detention centres set up in Morocco to hold
Africans 'suspected of wanting to cross into Spain'. In 1993, 1,300
people were arrested in Cadiz trying to enter, 164 on small boats.
1993: reform of asylum law makes criteria stricter, limits rights of
rejected asylum-seekers, particularly those rejected at the border as

economic migrants. At same time, quota system linking immigration to the 'need for manual work in the economy' was put into place.

October 1993: Broad anti-deportation coalition formed after the removal by deception of ten Moroccan children who were not given the chance to claim asylum.

February 1994: judges condemn conditions in 'model' immigration detention centre at Malaga where detainees are held for up to forty days.

Racism and fascism

Legislation: New law of 1993 penalises racism or xenophobia against individuals. Criminal code allows compensation for discrimination; labour laws prohibit discrimination at work.

Electoral parties: No parliamentary extreme Right party but many organisations nostalgic for the return of the Franco era like CEDADE (1965) (SPANISH CIRCLE OF FRIENDS OF EUROPE), which organises the annual Franco parade, and, of course, the FALANGE. The FRENTE NATIONALE (1986), led by Blas Pinar, is probably the largest of the extreme Right parties and claims to have 1,000 councillors in Spain elected as independents.

Neo-nazi and skinhead violence organised by groups such as BASES AUTONOMAS. Following murder of Dominican worker, Lucrecia Perez, it emerged that three 16-year-old youths who participated in the killing were members of the Real Madrid Ultrasur supporters group (the other man arrested was a member of the civil guard). In January 1993, Football Anti-Violence Commission accused football clubs such as Real Madrid of refusing to clamp down on neo-nazi violence. Two killings by far Right in 1993.

Racial violence: Attacks on Romanies and immigrant workers becoming more commonplace in 1992-93. In June 1992, mayor of Fraga resigned after refusing to denounce an attack by thirty right-wingers on a hostel for north Africans. In October 1992, mayor and ten members of ruling council of Mancha Real jailed for their part in an attack in which six houses belonging to Romany families were burnt down by an angry mob. In summer 1993, a mob hounded north African seasonal workers out of a village in Lerida and 1,000 people tried to storm a Romany home in Valencia. A north African was beaten to death and his body thrown from the Malaga-Madrid train by racists.

Police: Much harassment of foreigners following new security laws to deal with illegal immigrants and constant identity checks on black people. For instance, a police attack on a black American musician who refused to produce his passport quickly enough left him with severe facial injuries, including a broken nose, and led to the cancellation of his television appearance. A Moroccan man had to have a testicle removed after a severe beating by Valencia police in March 1992.

SWEDEN (EFTA, EEA, Nordic Union; has applied to join EU)

Population: 8.6m

Basis of citizenship: By descent, though those born in Sweden of foreign parents may apply to register. Naturalisation possible with five years' residence, good conduct (no convictions during qualifying period). Nordic citizens need only two years' residence.

Immigration and asylum

Asylum-seekers: 37,600 in 1993 (reduced from 80,000 in 1992); 76 per cent from former Yugoslavia, the rest from Iraq, Somalia, Uganda, Peru, ex-Soviet Union.

Law and practice: 1992: refugee reception centres 'function like open prisons' according to report; asylum-seekers' living allowances cut by 5-10 per cent. Proposals to privatise refugee reception centres, to limit 'de facto' refugees by strict quota dependent on demands of labour market, and to make deportation easier.

1993: revision of asylum law announced to abolish 'de facto' status. One hundred and forty-one lawyers complained publicly of severity of refugee procedures, which they said excluded victims of torture. UNHCR criticised government for apparent blanket policy of rejection and return of Kosovo Albanians. Plans to repatriate Tamils to Sri Lanka announced.

1994: between 85 and 95 per cent of rejected asylum-seekers are deported, the highest figure in Europe. Government commission recommends deportation of non-Convention refugees convicted of petty crime (breach of peace, shoplifting). From 1 July, asylum-seekers will have to work to get allowance.

Racism and fascism

Legislation: Has Ombudsman for race discrimination complaints.

Electoral parties: SVERIGE DEMOKRATERNA (Swedish Democrats, 1988), led by Anders Klarstrom. Anti-immigration electoral party which has failed to make a significant impact at parliamentary level. In September 1992 general election, it won 5,000 votes, which represents the largest vote for a fascist party since the second world war. NEW DEMOCRATS, led by Ian Wachtmeister until his resignation in February 1994.

Other parties: VIT ARISKT MOTSTÅND (VAM – White Aryan Resistance) responsible for a wave of bombings and attacks throughout Sweden. Although no official connection with Swedish Democrats, VAM members have acted as their stewards on demonstrations. Known to be involved in organised crime and to be armed, they are linked to STORM NETWORK, an informal network which binds together Sweden's top neo-nazis.

Racial violence: Trial ended January 1994 with life imprisonment for 'laser man', a maverick racist gunman who carried out a series of attacks against immigrants in late 1991 and early 1992, killing one man and seriously injuring at least ten others. 1993: attackers of Somali who suffered severe brain damage after their assault received sentences ranging from two to thirty-four months.

SWITZERLAND (EFTA; rejected membership of EEA)

Population: 6.8m (non-citizens 1,200,000, of whom one-third are non-EU/EFTA).

Basis of citizenship: By descent, adoption. Naturalisation based on twelve years' residence and integration, very difficult. December 1993: Bill to facilitate naturalisation by 'second generation immigrants' approved by parliament.

Immigration and asylum

Asylum-seekers: 24,700 in 1993, most from former Yugoslavia and Somalia.

Law and practice: Immigration limited to temporary, seasonal and border workers (with EU and EFTA workers favoured) and to refugees. No freedom of movement between cantons for asylum-seekers. Fast screening of asylum-seekers, centralised decisions, army occasionally deployed to help border police on eastern border. Wage deductions levied from those in work to pay for their possible deportation.

1992: reception centre staff instructed to refuse registration to asylum-seekers without ID documents. Plans to deter asylum-seekers further included repatriation assistance and information campaigns in countries of origin, greater powers of detention and internment, use of military barracks. New prison approved at Klonten airport (Zurich) for refused asylum-seekers, deportees. December 1993: visa requirement imposed on Bosnian refugees. January 1994: government signed accord with Sri Lanka to enable forced repatriation of Tamils. Announcement of plan to repatriate Kosovo Albanians.

Racism and fascism
Legislation: New law imminent against race discrimination, in line with plan to ratify UN Covenant against Racial Discrimination. New penal law bans denial of holocaust.
Electoral parties: No far-Right electoral party as such, but the Swiss DEMOCRATS (formerly National Action), who have five seats on the National Council, are known for their anti-immigrant stance. The anti-communist AUTOMOBILE PARTY, which has eight seats on the National Council, is associated with campaigns against asylum-seekers.
Other parties: Many small neo-nazi parties like the PATRIOTIC FRONT, the NATIONALE AKTION FUR VOLK UND HEIMAT and the NATIONALE SOZIALISTISCHE PARTEI known to have been involved in attacks on refugee centres. In October 1993, ACTION FOR FREE SPEECH presented a 50,000-strong petition demanding a plebiscite to repeal the UN Convention Against Racial Discrimination.
Racial violence: In 1992, two deaths of refugees resulted from numerous attacks, including arson and petrol bombings, on refugee centres. Police denied racial motivation, putting it down to 'drunken behaviour'.

UNITED KINGDOM (EU)
Population: 56.7m (2.7m non-citizens). 29,000 Turks, 148,000 Africans, 72,000 Caribbeans and central/south Americans, 453,000 Asians.
Basis of citizenship: By descent; by birth in UK to parent with permanent residence; naturalisation based on five years' residence (three years for those married to British citizens), character, language. Five types of 'British overseas' citizenship for former colonial subjects which confer no residence rights in Britain.

Immigration and asylum
Asylum-seekers: 16,700 Jan-Sept 1993, mainly from former Yugoslavia, Turkey, Ghana, Somalia, Sri Lanka and Nigeria: 7.2 per cent accepted, 52 per cent granted 'exceptional leave to remain'.
Law and practice: Strict laws restrict immigration to family reunion (for entry of spouses, proof demanded of motives for marriage). Visa controls and carrier sanctions to restrict entry of asylum-seekers. Unlimited detention of asylum-seekers in prisons and detention centres. 1992: number of asylum-seekers was halved as thousands were returned to 'safe third countries' through which they had come.

1993: new Asylum and Immigration Appeals Act withdraws rights of appeal for some categories of immigrants, introduces fast-track processing for 'manifestly unfounded' claims, gives rejected asylum-seekers two to fourteen days to appeal, imposes compulsory fingerprinting on asylum-seekers and reduces their housing rights. Rate of refusal of asylum and of exceptional leave to remain increases dramatically after new law comes into force.

November 1993: new immigration detention centre opened at Campsfield, outside Oxford. December 1993: 190 Jamaicans detained on arrival on UK tour, and twenty-seven deported on special charter flight on Xmas day. March 1994: increased use of detention of asylum-seekers, and higher rejection and removal rate, led to hunger strike which spreads to 200 detainees in detention centres and prisons throughout England.

Racism and fascism

Legislation: Laws against race discrimination and incitement to racial hatred.

Electoral parties: No electoral party of any note, but the small, openly neo-nazi BRITISH NATIONAL PARTY put up candidates in the 1992 general election with little success (as did the even smaller NATIONAL FRONT). The BNP has built up a base in certain areas of white discontent, notably in east London where it won its first ever local council seat in September 1993.

The BLOOD AND HONOUR movement mobilises young neo-nazis, mostly skinheads, around racist music bands. The distributors of SKREWDRIVER SERVICES were recently sent to prison for incitement to racial hatred. Most recently, a group called COMBAT 18 or REDWATCH has emerged – its main aim being to harass 'left' targets.

Racial violence: Widespread racial violence across the country. In 1992, ten people died in racially motivated incidents, including two refugees. In 1993, three people were killed in racist attacks. Research by the London Research Centre indicates that one in ten ethnic minority households in London has suffered racial harassment, and Home Office minister Peter Lloyd agreed that there could be over 140,000 incidents of racial harassment per year.

Police: Much concern over police methods of interrogation and the failure of the criminal justice system to provide safeguards following the release of both Irish and black prisoners who have served long sentences for crimes they did not commit. Police had to pay out record sums to the victims of miscarriages of justice in 1992 and 1993. The death of Joy Gardner in August 1993, after her mouth was taped and she was restrained by a body belt during an attempted deportation, revealed the existence of a special deportation squad.

Institutional violence: An alarming number of black deaths in police cells, prisons and special hospitals. In 1993, the inquest into the death of Zairean asylum seeker Omasase Lumumba revealed disturbing evidence of institutionalised violence at Pentonville prison. It concluded that Lumumba had been unlawfully killed. Two black men killed themselves after being subjected to institutional racism in 1993: one had been refused asylum, another had been arrested for carrying a weapon to protect himself against racist attacks.